Praise for
STiCKY NoTE MANTRAS

"Stuck in a negative headspace? *Sticky Note Mantras* provides tools to shift into a healthy mindset and the self-regulation skills to sustain it. Helene and Beth create an empowering place for readers to improve negative patterns of thinking to achieve a more fulfilling outlook on life! This is a relatable read for any individual looking to gain insight into a more positive outlook."

—Shannon Francis, LCSW and owner of Well Therapy, PLLC

"From the moment I picked up *Sticky Note Mantras*, I was completely captivated and couldn't put it down. At first, I expected simple words of affirmation and mindset changes, but what I found was so much more—a powerful guide filled with practical steps, attention-grabbing pictures, and wonderful quotes that inspire real change and personal growth. The chapter 'Just Breathe, Damn It!' truly hit home. Breathing is the first thing we do at birth and the last thing we do at life's end, making it a profound journey all on its own. This book dives deep into various breathing techniques and their incredible psychological benefits, such as lowering blood pressure, reducing stress, and boosting serotonin and dopamine. If you're on a quest for a book that tackles every aspect of self-awareness and self-care, *Sticky Note Mantras* is your ultimate companion on the path to becoming the best version of yourself. Get ready to transform your life!"

—Herbert Decker Jr. III, author of *Coach. Heal. Motivate.: Coach the mind, heal the body, and motivate the spirit!*

"Helene and Beth take us on a journey through the neurological and psychological components behind the power of our thoughts. *Sticky Note Mantras* presents a new, positive solution to redirect unhealthy thoughts. The book is laced with warmth, humor, and simple mantras to let go of the clutter of our minds. It's a good book to read over and over to help us change our thoughts, which inevitably will change our lives."

—Pamela Chambers, MEd, NBCC,
author of *My Mommy's Getting Married*

"This book promises to help you break free from the constraints of your thoughts by using the authors' tried-and-true technique—mantras. For readers who want to move beyond negative and counterproductive thinking in daily life, *Sticky Note Mantras* offers a solution. Colorfully told through personal stories, an explanation of the underlying rationale, and lists of actual mantras to try, Helene Zupanc and Beth Valdez present a practical guide to this form of deliberate refocusing. Approach-ably written and thoroughly entertaining, the chapters describe common mental obstacles and offer mantras, well-known songs, and further resources to combat them. If you want a kickstart to having a more positive inner dialogue, *Sticky Note Mantras* is for you."

—Jennifer E. Hassel, author of *Badass Grief*

"*Sticky Note Mantras* is a wonderful tool for anyone with a goal to move toward positive life changes. Helene and Beth provide a useful, humorous, relatable, hands-on guide to self-reflection and personal growth. Openly and honestly, the authors share their own life experiences and individual quests toward self-reflection and improvement in all areas of their lives. Using personal anecdotes, they help to guide and support the reader in their own adventure of self-discovery and evolution toward positive change. *Sticky Note Mantras* provides practical techniques to encourage and motivate the reader in a fun and nonthreatening manner. So, I encourage you to use this valuable tool to move toward personal discovery and growth! 'Be the water, not the rock.' Let the journey begin!"

—Shelley Ratliff, MSCP, therapist and life coach

"Helene Ann Zupanc and Beth G. Valdez set a clear, easy roadmap on how to think differently, shift thoughts, and reset reasoning to choose mindful management through their motivational mantras. The human framework in *Sticky Note Mantras* channels positivity and awareness everyone can apply daily; specifically, there is no 'one-size-fits-all' approach to emotions and life. We can all be trapped in our self-imposed thinking in search of the correct compass direction. As we navigate life, *Sticky Note Mantras* presents beneficial techniques, inspirational quotes, alternate mantras, song playlists, and further reading articles that support specific mantras that are enlightening. What an enriching life resource!"

—Letitia (Tish) E. Hart, deacon and author of *Reach Out with Acts of Kindness: A Guide to Helping Others in Crisis*

"As a retired elementary school teacher, parent, and grandparent who is forever learning and searching for new ideas that help me grow, I found a wealth of information in *Sticky Note Mantras*. I felt like I was sitting in on a course in modern psychology, being presented with all the latest data and given relevant ideas, references, quotes, and songs on how to use it. In the margins, I was writing mantras to go with almost every sentence! A great book for friends, family, educators, and retirees. After you've absorbed the book, you can go to the references and continue reading!"

—Donna Hodgson, Ft. Collins, Colorado

"I love the way the authors speak to the reader like an old friend catching up over a cup of coffee."

—Betsy Torrens, Homdel, New Jersey

"Throughout much of my professional journey, my focus has been working with adolescents and adults grappling with substance use disorder. My experience spans beyond clinical work to encompass program development and administration. Among the prevailing themes among our patients are negative thought patterns, low self-esteem, and distorted cognition, often compounded by histories of trauma and pervasive anxiety. While many therapeutic resources are tailored for trained professionals, *Sticky Note Mantras* breaks the mold. This book strikes a unique balance of wit, levity, and profound insight, making it accessible to all readers. With its engaging approach, *Sticky Note Mantras* tackles complex topics such as self-worth and negative thinking with ease and humor. Its practical exercises, memorable quotes, and relatable anecdotes facilitate tangible progress in a remarkably short span. In my recent implementation of this book within group therapy sessions, I've witnessed remarkable transformations in my clients' attitudes and behaviors. I wholeheartedly endorse *Sticky Note Mantras* not only for its practicality but also for its delightful humor. Authors Beth Valdez and Helene Zupanc have masterfully combined their expertise with a playful perspective on life. I highly recommend this book not only to therapists and clinicians but to anyone seeking personal growth and self-improvement."

—Dori Haddock, LCSW, Arkansas

"*Sticky Note Mantras* offers therapeutic skills and inspiration one mantra at a time for those who like to approach personal growth at their own pace. It is fun to read; when something sparks your interest, you find yourself curious and wanting more. Additional resources are provided to help you continue the journey. Thank you, Beth and Helene. I am growing into a better person."

—Paula H, Colorado

Sticky Note Mantras:
The Art and Science of Choosing Your Thoughts

by Helene Ann Zupanc & Beth G. Valdez

© Copyright 2024 Helene Ann Zupanc & Beth G. Valdez

ISBN 979-8-88824-355-8

All rights reserved. No part of this publication may be reproduced, stored in a retrieval system, or transmitted in any form or by any means—electronic, mechanical, photocopy, recording, or any other—except for brief quotations in printed reviews, without the prior written permission of the author.

Published by

◂köehlerbooks™

3705 Shore Drive
Virginia Beach, VA 23455
800-435-4811
www.koehlerbooks.com

STICKY NOTE MANTRAS

The Art and Science of Choosing Your Thoughts

STICKY NOTE MANTRAS

The Art and Science of Choosing Your Thoughts

Helene Ann Zupanc
& Beth G. Valdez

VIRGINIA BEACH
CAPE CHARLES

TABLE OF CONTENTS

INTRODUCTION 1

PART I: THE ART AND SCIENCE OF CHOOSING YOUR THOUGHTS

A CONVERSATION ABOUT THE ART
Habits are Frikin' Powerful 9

REALLY IMPORTANT MANTRA STUFF
Awareness Is Key 18
It's Go Time—Guide to Creating Your Own Mantras 26
Make It Your Own—Personalize, Expand, and Implement 31
Closing 35

BETH AND HELENE'S PERSONAL MANTRA STORIES 37

PART II: MANTRAS FOR EVERYDAY OBSTACLES

RAINY DAY MANTRAS 47

TOPIC	MANTRA
• Perfectionism	Imperfection Is Beauty 48
• Positive Self-Concept	Believe 59
• Laughter as Medicine	Humor Is Healing 68
• Rediscovering Your Curiosity	Be Curious 75
• Inner Strength	You Can Do Hard Things 83

MANTRAS THAT ENCOURAGE LETTING GO 92

TOPIC	MANTRA
• Letting Go & Living Simply	If It's Not OK, It's Not the End 93
• Perceptions	Assumptions Are Assholes 103
• Acceptance	Let Reality Be Reality 112
• Forgiveness	Forgive & Make Room 121

MANTRAS TO INSPIRE ACTION.. 130

TOPIC	MANTRA
• Taking Action & Goal-Setting	Just Don't Stand Still............ 131
• Being Present & Mindful Meditation	Leave Your Mind Behind 138
• Gratitude	Focus on the Good 147
• Balance	Mix It Up 156

MANTRAS ABOUT SELF-CARE.. 164

TOPIC	MANTRA
• Self-Care	Self-care is Not Self-Indulgence It's Self-preservation............ 165
• Self-Compassion	Include YOU in Kindness.... 177
• Breathwork	Just Breathe, Damn It 186
• Introspection	Talk to Your Soul................ 194
• Mind-Body Connection	Mind and Body: BFFs 202

Dedication

HELENE:
To my mom, who has been there for me every step of the way and *always* has time for a mantra brainstorming session. And my dad, whose love, guidance, and humor live on within me. To my husband and son, the Franks, who always believe in me even when I don't believe in myself. And to my coauthor, Beth, your humor, friendship, and compassion absolutely light up my life.

BETH:
To my children, who are a piece of my heart out exploring the world, you inspire me to be better and to make the world a better place. To my partner in crime, Douglas, who still makes me laugh and encourages me to keep moving forward. I'm grateful to have you by my side.

I will always be eternally grateful to my mom, dad, and sister, who selflessly put their lives on hold to care for my family and me when we could not do so.

Finally, to my coauthor Helene, I honestly have never met a kinder soul. Your unwavering belief in the goodness of others continues to amaze me, as does your courage, strength, and fantastic sense of humor. Thank you for being you.

INTRODUCTION

"Emancipate yourself from mental slavery.
None but ourselves can free our minds."
—Bob Marley

Why is changing the way we think so hard? It's like playing the banjo as you climb Mt. Kilimanjaro while wearing stilettos and trying to solve integrative calculus problems. Feels impossible! Yes, changing our ingrained thought patterns has historically proven to be a real pain in the ass. The cause behind this ultimate challenge to our health and well-being is none other than our most complex, ingenious, and mysterious organ: ladies and gentlemen, let's hear it for your brain! It makes sure that once we've gotten into a particular way of thinking, things *don't* change. Change is a bad word to your brain. Forget fuck, shit, fuck shitters, and all that; the word *change* is what offends our brain! Yup, thoughts that have long outlived their purpose are strangely difficult to let go of. You know, the ones about perfectionism, what we *should* be doing, rumination, procrastination, shame, regret, self-doubt, etc. So, it is not at all surprising that many people feel stuck and locked into old thought patterns.

What happens when we shout "*carpe diem*" to the world and decide to implement a shiny, new positive thought? We start off good for a few days, only to slip right back into the old Negative Nancy thinking routine. The body and brain always seek out the path of least resistance because they're efficient little bastards when it comes to our immediate survival. In other words, our brain will always take the easy route, and since change is hard, it's certainly not going to veer onto the more challenging route without a fight. Just like muscle memory, our brain shifts into autopilot whenever it gets a chance. This is an ingrained survival mechanism to conserve energy so we can survive the moment. During autopilot, we are no longer choosing our thoughts. Our brain automatically chooses them for us, even if those thoughts are skewed or unhelpful. What's really messed up about all of this is we go right along believing those crazy thoughts, drinking our brain's special purple Kool-Aid.

We invite you to embark on a wild journey to break free from the constraints of your thoughts with a simple yet highly effective secret weapon: mantras! Let us be your entertaining but informative guides as we encourage you to stop believing your thoughts and start choosing them. We know you will love this inspirational process. The joy of using mantras taps into really good and fun stuff, like your creativity, preferences, and style. It heightens your awareness, encourages you to craft the thoughts you want, and weaves these new thoughts into your brain so they stick. You'll discover how to tune in with those thoughts rolling through your head and listen to them without *being* them. Then, you can begin to ignore the ones you don't want and choose the ones that best serve you. Once you learn this process, you'll find it mind-boggling that you let your brain run the show for so long. That bossy little bastard needs to be kept in check. Just a little heads up: mantras are not a panacea or magic wand. Change takes time and practice, just like anything worthwhile.

This book has two main sections. Part I, "The Art and Science of Choosing Your Thoughts," gives background information about mantras. It includes the definition, the rationale, and techniques that support their use. Part II, "Mantras for Everyday Obstacles," explores ready-made mantras supplemented with rich inspiration and sound information. This section overflows with mental health topics such as breathwork, goal setting, forgiveness, self-care, gratitude, humor, and so much more.

At the end of each chapter, there are exercises for you to try on. Yes, *try on* because not all the exercises will resonate with you. It's a bit like art. For some, Jackson Pollack is a genius; for others, he just splatters paint on the canvas. You know, beauty in the eye of the beholder and all that stuff. So, take a few of these for a test drive and see what fits you best. To further personalize each topic, we have listed alternate mantras, quotes, songs, and resources at the end of each chapter.

Mantras have been an integral part of our lives; we use them every single day. They get us through tough spots and the daily bullshit. We have utilized them professionally, working with individuals of all ages from all walks of life in our careers as therapists, school counselors, and teachers. It is our sincerest hope that using mantras, along with some colorful sticky notes, will inspire others to live happier, healthier lives and have some fun while they're doing it.

Namaste,

Beth & Helene

PART 1:
The Art and Science of Choosing Your Thoughts

A CONVERSATION ABOUT THE ART

> **Sticky Note Mantras**
> ## Habits Are Frickin' Powerful

"Don't believe everything you hear—even in your own mind."
—Daniel G. Amen

Q: What's the Art of Choosing My Thoughts? I Thought I Was Already Choosing Them.
You've been thinking, but that doesn't mean you've been choosing. The art of choosing your thoughts involves becoming aware of your thoughts, and that, our friends, is where the magic happens. *That's* where a conscious choice exists. We want the option to choose our thoughts because thoughts are not reality; they are just one interpretation the brain spits out. Often, they are skewed or flat-out wrong. But we believe them because they are a product of (dun, dun, dun ...) habit. *Habits are frickin' powerful.* The longer you think a certain way, the more automatic it becomes. Even if a thought is untrue, its existence changes how you feel, react, and behave. That's why, together, we'll be taking some time to pause and reflect. These pauses will give us an opportunity to examine our thoughts and their influence over us.

The brain is a busy little beaver, constantly processing and interpreting a high volume of information streaming in from the world around us. Some of it is pretty straightforward, but *a lot* is muddled up in that gray abyss somewhere in between. So, to compensate for the unknown, our brain makes sense of it all by guessing and filling in the blanks. Because our brains are wired for survival and self-protection, these guesses are often exaggerated projections of fears and insecurities, including worries about being  unloved, unsafe, unworthy, or not enough. Our brains engage in this weaving of tall tales because it feels safer to know than not to know. Yes, our brains can come to some pretty wild, unhelpful, and even harmful conclusions. These narratives typically begin in childhood or adolescence and then solidify in early adulthood. Dr. Brené Brown, an icon in the field of mental health and well-being, wrote about the human need to create stories in her book *Rising Strong: The Reckoning, the Rumbling, the Revolution*: "In the absence of data, we will always make up stories. In fact, the need to make up a story, especially when we are hurt, is part of our most primitive survival wiring. Meaning making is in our biology, and our default is often to come up with a story that makes sense, feels familiar, and offers us insight into how best to self-protect." Yes! We humans are meaning-making machines! We repeat the same stories to ourselves again and again because they are familiar, which our brains love, love, love! Even when we want to change, they have an uncanny way of sticking around and causing problems. Never fear; we will work on updating these stories together.

We're sure you have heard the saying *your thoughts cause your feelings*; well, it's absolutely true. You may think your feelings are related to "good" or "bad" things that happen to you. You get a flat tire, and you're upset. You get a promotion at work, and you're proud. But really, it's your *perception* of what happens that causes your feelings. If situations caused feelings, then everyone would react the same way to every situation. Epictetus, the philosopher and scientist, said, "It's not the events of life that change us emotionally; it's the way we view those things in life." So, yes, the narratives we tell ourselves are more influential than the actual events. Acknowledging these stories our minds make up is the premise of Cognitive Behavioral Therapy (CBT): change your thoughts and change your brain. Take back your power! You have options; you don't have to believe everything you think.

Q: Why Can't I Just Pick Different Thoughts?

If only it were that easy. Picking new thoughts is a lot harder than it sounds! Thoughts are tough to change because, again, they are a product of habit. We've said it before, and we'll say it again: habits are tremendously powerful. Deepak Chopra and David Simon illustrate this point beautifully in the following passage in their book, *Grow Younger, Live Longer:*

> If a rope is tied around the leg of a baby elephant and attached to a stake in the ground, it learns that it can only move within very narrow limits. Years later, as a powerful adult, it remains within narrow confines when its leg is staked, even though it has the strength to uproot the entire tree. It has been conditioned to accept the limitation imposed upon it. In a similar way, most people think and act within the narrow limitations of what they have been taught during childhood, without questioning the basic assumptions that structure their worldview. To live a healthier, richer, more creative life, you need to recognize that most of what you hold to be true derives from habits of thought.

Hell yeah, and damn straight! Habits are so compelling that they shape our lives. Additionally, our past traumas—the major ones and tiny ones, often referred to as big Ts and little ts—influence our thought patterns. Our brain remembers any little event that has caused us physical or emotional pain and holds onto them like a jackpot-winning lottery ticket. When a situation triggers anything associated with one of our traumas, the brain switches into survival mode, and that's where the fun begins. Fight, flight, or freeze, baby, all systems go! So, not only are we fighting our ingrained thought patterns, but we are also going toe-to-toe with our past traumas. We can't stress this enough: *address your past traumas*. It's critical for moving forward. The old adage "what you don't repair, you repeat" holds true! Mantras can certainly help you tackle your traumas, but they work best with combined therapeutic experiences. For example, work with a therapist, research, journal, spend time in nature, join a group, or reach out to a spiritual advisor. Or try alternative therapies such as massage or acupuncture or an introspective journey à la Cheryl Strayed in *Wild*.

Q: How can we make change happen?
Now that we know *why* we want to choose our thoughts, let's explore *how* we can make these changes. We usually can grapple with the *why*: why our health needs to make changes, such as losing weight, being less anxious, having more self-compassion, or being grateful. It's the *how* that trips us up. So, we begin to collect more information. We browse the internet, listen to podcasts, and watch informational shows. Essentially, we start a quest to gather as much "how-to" information as we can, and then . . . drumroll . . . we continue to do the same shit we've always done. Change is elusive because most of us do not know *how* to practice thinking differently. If we compare our brains to an old-fashioned computer, the issue lies in the computer's difficulty with transferring information. We receive continuous error messages when downloading new data because our brains have been hardwired to think the same way they've always thought, and it is not programmed to accept and adapt to change easily. So, when we try to change and apply stuff we've learned, our minds go back to automatic pilot, leading us to repeat the same thoughts and behaviors.

Consider this scenario: you've just read a great article on healthy eating, exercising, or parenting, and you're eager to make changes. You implement a few things the first day or two but then slip back into your routine, and the plan about changing flies right out the window. Sound familiar? *You're not alone.* Humans love to revert to what's familiar and comfortable, *especially* in times of stress, which is pretty much all the damn time, right? Your brain says, *Yeah, sooo . . . about changing . . . I'm not really up for that. We will go ahead and use the good old standby coping strategies. I don't care if they're batshit crazy and unhelpful as all get out. It's just sooooo much easier for me.* This phenomenon is why it takes hard work and practice to actually *use* the wisdom and insights we acquire.

The good news is that by continually replacing limiting thoughts with healthy beliefs, we can eventually rewire our brains, leading to more permanent change. What we need is an effective strategy to interrupt old cycles of thought, help the mind focus on a new direction, and then repeat the message. *Mantras are a simple yet profoundly effective tactic to do just that.* The repetitive nature and conciseness of mantras make them ideal vehicles to replace negative thoughts with more inspiring and lighthearted ones. Mantras are about healthy mind management, moving away from the traditional and outdated medical model, which treats mental health as a disease that needs to be diagnosed and fixed. The entire process of creating and using mantras digs out the roots of unhealthy habits and slowly replaces them with more constructive ones. In other words, mantras foster a healthy, holistic, mindful lifestyle.

Q: Is There Proof That Mantras Work?
There is overwhelming evidence that mantras are wildly effective! In the past, limited resources were available to evaluate the effectiveness of therapeutic interventions. Previous studies regarding changes to our thought process were very subjective. Today, there's sophisticated brain-scanning technology, such as PET (positron-emission

tomography) and SPECT (single photon emission computed tomography). It's now possible to monitor chemical changes in the brain and scientifically evaluate the effectiveness of interventions. Science has proven that we forge new neural pathways and synaptic connections by redirecting our thoughts with cognitive strategies such as mantras. Practicing these strategies alters our brain chemistry and can override our genetic predispositions. Researchers have shown that the process of awareness and refocusing relaxes the brain. It also can reduce freak-outs, anxiety, depression, and all kinds of things you don't want in your life. Using awareness combined with mantras as a mind management tool overrides negative programming and helps your brain update and forge new neural pathways. These new positive pathways will improve how you feel and your overall outlook.

Q: What Exactly Is a Mantra?
Mantras are short phrases that guide us and focus our intentions. They are the path to channeling purpose, direction, and affirmations into the mind. We like Webster's definition: *a mystical formula of invocation or incantation.* Yes! Mantras encourage the wise counselor inside of you to speak up and set you straight when the brain goes rogue with its emotional and irrational thinking. Mantras date back thousands of years from the Sanskrit language, the classical language of India, and the ceremonial language of Hinduism and Buddhism. The word mantra comes from the root "man," which means to think, and "tra," meaning to liberate. Combined, it means to liberate yourself from thought. Letting go of thoughts is freeing! Long ago, the most critical components of a mantra involved meaning and sound or vibration. In Hinduism, *Aum* is known as the first sound created, and the vibration of which brought everything into existence. It is chanted as a mantra to feel a connection with the universe in many Eastern practices. Today, mantras are widely recognized as any statement that inspires us or affirms how we want to live our lives.

Q: Why Is It So Difficult to Change?
That's a loaded question! Here's an abbreviated answer: it takes years for your thought pattern to evolve unconsciously. Humans start with a "tabula rasa"—or clean slate—as babies. One thought builds upon the next, forming our perspective. Our experiences, such as past traumas, successes, failures, familial upbringing, and connections, are central to every person's complicated and unique self. Throw in genetics and generational traumas, and you've got the whole enchilada. *Changing* patterns of ingrained behavior is much more complicated than starting from scratch. The inspirational author Gary Ryan Blair perfectly illustrates this point: "Learning is about more than simply acquiring new knowledge and insights; it is also crucial to unlearn old knowledge that has outlived its relevance. Thus, forgetting is probably at least as important as learning." Even if you tell your brain to forget old ways of thinking, it has a mysterious way of remembering. This is our survival mechanism at work again. Your brain repeats unhelpful inner dialogue as a form of protection. Reprogramming negative thoughts is a lifelong task due to our deep conditioning; mantras are the perfect way to break the cycle!

Q: But Is It Even Possible?
We won't sugarcoat it; change of any kind takes time, belief, and work, but it is certainly possible! The good news is that mantras will make the work much easier and, dare we say, fun? When you have an insight or learn something new, it creates a neural pathway in your brain. New pathways do not last long if they are not supported and repeated. Think about when you study for a test; you can hold the information in your mind until the day of the test but then forget it if you no longer think about it or use it in day-to-day life. In academia, they refer to this as the *forgetting curve*. If you do not practice or review the information you want to retain, your brain efficiently weeds out the unused neural pathway, making room for storing new information.

Again, the brain does this because survival is its number one goal. Why should a student remember the dates of the American Revolution if they don't need it to get by every day? The brain consistently trims up what it feels is nonessential just in case more important information comes along. Lasting change is made possible only when we consistently practice and integrate new habits into our routines. The longer a thought is repeated, the stronger the pathway becomes. Mantras interrupt the gravitation toward your old thought processes, helping you "unlearn" your previous patterns and create more robust pathways that stick. Essentially, mantras help you to make the same choice every day and reinforce new pathways in the brain until they become more automatic. Whether there's a big change you want to make or some small positive ideas you want to integrate into your life, mantras will help you on your way, peeps!

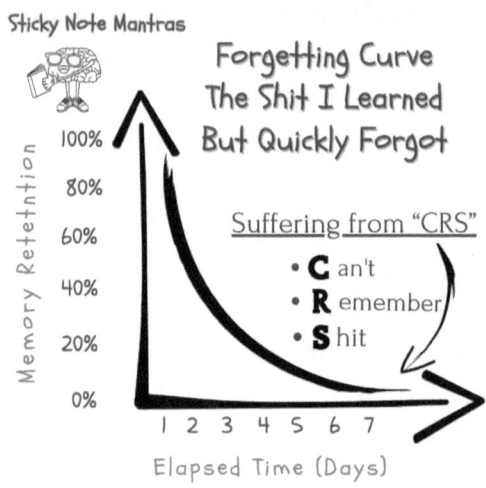

✷ It's Your Turn to Play, Learn, and Explore ✷

This section is included at the end of each chapter to help put the concepts you learned into practice. With that being said, there is no "one-size-fits-all" approach when it comes to our brains. So, please feel free to modify the exercises to make them just right for you!

Putting Your Thoughts on Trial

This exercise is often used in CBT. You have the honor of being a no-holds-barred defense attorney, relentless prosecutor, and no-nonsense judge to determine the accuracy of one of your thoughts by gathering evidence for and against it. Facts only! No bullshit, guesses, emotional thinking, opinions, interpretations, conjectures, or perjury allowed! This keeps the brain's storytelling in check and pulls in the logical part of the brain to do some assumption-checking. There's role-playing going on, so get ready to dial up the creativity and visualize a courtroom scene. The key players are the thought, the defense, the prosecution, and the judge. You are the plaintiff in this trial. The defendant is your unhelpful thought. If the thought is convicted, you'll brainstorm a more balanced thought! Here's an example:

The Thought in Question:
Everyone at work thinks I'm an idiot. I suck.

The Defense (evidence):
I screwed up and didn't handle a situation well at work. When I make a mistake, people no longer like me, respect me, or think I'm good at my job.

The Prosecution (evidence against your thought):
This is just one incident. Overall, I'm good at my job and am not an idiot every day. Most people at my work know that I have good intentions and would not try to cause discomfort. They can always talk to me if they're upset, and I can elaborate. I am building this up in my mind, and they might not even know what the heck I am talking about if I bring it up. Everyone is human, including the people I work with.

The Judge's Verdict:
Con-fucking-victed! [The gavel hits the desk: Bang! Bang!] Order in the courtroom! It's high time to let this thought go because rumination will only make it more powerful.

The bailiffs struggle to take your thought away. All the other thoughts in the courtroom go wild! It's mayhem!

REALLY IMPORTANT MANTRA STUFF

"In the process of observing your own mind, you embark on the greatest job ever: using the mind to look in upon itself."
—DONALD ALTMAN, *The Mindfulness Code*

Q: IS AWARENESS A Needed Ingredient in Using Mantras?
Hell yeah! Practicing awareness, or mindfulness, is a *vital* ingredient in maximizing the benefits of using mantras to shift to healthier thoughts. If you like to highlight important stuff in books, here's the place to do it: *Awareness is the key that brings limiting thoughts and narratives into your conscious mind.* Our minds are constantly buzzing with tons of thoughts. They just happen; autopilot is *on*, baby! We would not want to be aware of the millions of little connections that go into our thoughts; that would drive us all insane. But we do have to start honing in on *some* thoughts, especially the ones that no longer serve us, which is more than you might think! According to the National Science Foundation, we think over 50,000 thoughts per day. More than 80 percent are negative, and 90 percent are repeats from

the day before. That's a lot of unproductive, unhealthy, and downright detrimental thoughts.

Evolutionary-wise, these types of critical auto thoughts started as a way to scan our environment and fix things or get out of danger. Fast-forward to the present day, where there are not too many life-threatening situations, and it adds up to crappy mental health. Today, we're more likely to run into emotional crises rather than life-threatening ones. However, our brain still interprets them as an emergency and tries to protect us. Eckhart Tolle, spiritual leader and self-help guru, talks about all of this negativity going on in our minds: "As it is, I would say about 80 to 90 percent of most people's thinking is not only repetitive and useless, but because of its dysfunctional and often negative nature, much of it is also harmful. Observe your mind and you will find this to be true. It causes a serious leakage of vital energy." Like he said, *observe your mind*. This check-in empowers you to shift your thinking when your brain is going down an unproductive path. You're going to love this whole process. You'll feel lighter, freer, and more able to influence your feelings and actions.

Q: Is Awareness a New Concept?
The concept of mindfulness is nothing new. It is sage wisdom practiced in Eastern cultures for thousands of years. The famous Greek philosopher Socrates was a mindfulness advocate and set the stage for what we know today as critical thinking. The process of critical thinking involves the ability to acknowledge and evaluate previous assumptions even when they seem to serve our best interests at the moment. Socrates was joined throughout the centuries by plenty of others, including Plato, Aristotle, Thomas Aquinas, Descartes, and John Locke, to name a few. Simply put, these deep-thinking fellows urged us to be observant of our thoughts and then question the shit out of them. They agreed that awareness gives us the choice to challenge and redirect our thoughts.

Q: What Does Awareness Do for You?

Awareness leads to those magical moments where detachment occurs. Detachment means pausing, stepping back, and acting as an outside observer. When you're not so enmeshed in your thoughts and feelings, it removes your mind's emotional involvement. This moment of pause is when you can access the autopilot off switch and override the system. For example, if you are struggling with a project at work or home, take a moment to become aware of what you are telling yourself. Are you saying *I can't do this?* Now is your big moment! Insert a mantra, such as *I can do hard things*, to counter your mind's unhelpful thoughts. It's also important to take moments where you stop trying to figure anything out, manage your life, or control anything. Your mantra can be: *Letting go, letting go, letting go.* Controlling situations through our thoughts is based on our fears. If you are a fellow overthinker, you know that constant thoughts cause anxiety and cloud your experience in the present moment. See the *Leave Your Mind Behind* mantra for more on this.

Neuroscience tells us that just like training our muscles to be more supple, we can coach our thinking to be more flexible. The capability to change our brain's hard wiring is called neuroplasticity. Remember those neural pathways? Neuroplasticity means you can shut down old pathways and create new ones through awareness and repetition. It's kind of like when you learned to drive. You were conscious of everything at first, such as keeping your hands at ten and two, looking left, right, left again, etc. After you did it a bunch of times, you were able to do it without thinking. In other words, the brain remembers stuff, like how to walk, brush your teeth, ride a bike, and add two numbers together, so you don't have to consciously figure it out each time. It's the same thing with your thought process; once you've been thinking the same way for a while, you do it unconsciously, forming the framework through which you see the world. It only becomes a problem when repeated thoughts are harmful to your well-being. Those problematic neural pathways are the ones we want to interrupt, shut down, and get off our autopilot repertoire. According to Dr. Caroline Leaf, a cognitive neuroscientist, "When we intentionally and deliberately direct our mind, we stimulate neuroplasticity in the brain and improve our functioning between 35 to 75 percent." Right on! The regular use of mantras allows you to reshape your brain like a little ball of putty.

Observing your mind also allows you to distinguish between different types of thoughts. The good ones are logical, rational, and fact-based. It's the irrational and emotional thoughts that need to go! These negative thoughts are the ones that have little to no evidence, but we go on thinking about them anyway. Irrational thoughts come in all shapes and sizes and are sometimes referred to as cognitive distortions, thinking errors, or, if you like a good rhyme, stinking thinking. Here's a list of the top five; we're sure you'll identify with at least a few of these because we all do them.

- **Catastrophizing**: Seeing only the worst possible outcome of the situation. *I'm going on a trip, and I'm sure I will get sick on the plane. Ahhhhh!*

- **Personalization**: Believing you're responsible for shit that's out of your control or taking things personally when they're not connected to you. *My son is having a hard time connecting with other kids at school. It's a reflection on me, and he could be doing better if I helped him more.*

- **Mind Reading**: Interpreting the thoughts and beliefs of others without evidence. You might also think that others are thinking the worst of you. *My spouse didn't give me a hug when I came home. He must be upset with me.*

- **Emotional Reasoning**: Assuming that your emotions reflect the way things really are. *I feel like I'm a bad mother, so I am a bad mother.*

- **Black-and-White Thinking:** Thinking in extremes or absolutes and using always/never a lot in your thoughts. *I never get anything done because I'm always running behind.*

Cognitive distortions are not our friends! They cause unwelcome chemical changes in our brains, such as depleting our serotonin and giving us a cortisol overload. We need to become aware of them and bust out some mantras before they take over our thinking and, ultimately, how we feel.

As you practice mindfulness, you will accomplish a perceptual shift in how you think and view the world around you. You will start recognizing your thoughts, emotions, and feelings as events you can observe. Thoughts will keep coming like waves crashing repeatedly. We don't need to stop them; we must let them roll on by. Then, we pause and use our mindfulness techniques to help us recognize them for what they truly are: unhelpful thoughts. Just like Jon Kabat-Zinn, the amazing mindfulness expert, said, "You can't stop the waves, but you can learn to surf!"

Q: Are There Techniques That Promote Awareness?

We are so glad you asked! There are plenty of techniques that will help you on your journey to becoming a mindful individual. Try these ideas on and see what fits you.

1. **Visual imagery** is a powerful technique in promoting awareness. It encourages you to separate from your thoughts instead of buying into or holding onto them. It involves brainstorming images of your thoughts as a separate entity from yourself. First, step outside yourself, like you are watching yourself. Then, try out some of the following images to see what best helps you distance yourself from your thoughts. Your thoughts are . . .

    - leaves floating down a river.
    - clouds dispersing in the sky.

- the wind blowing through tall trees.
- the ocean waves as they crash upon the sand.

Play around with images that help you remember that you are not your thoughts. Instead, think of them as ongoing background noise.

2. **Be aware of your body.** If you want to get in touch with your thoughts and feelings, checking in with your body is a perfect starting place. Recognize that the mind-body connection is always happening. Take a few moments to scan how you feel at different points of your body.
    - Are your shoulders tight and hunched up by your ears?
    - Is your stomach upset?
    - Do you have a tension headache?
    - Is your jaw clenched, or are you grinding your teeth?
    - Is your breathing shallow?

   Dr. George Sheehan, advocate of the mind-body connection, said, "The mind's first step to self-awareness must be through the body." You said it, George! Our bodies whisper so many cues, and if we don't listen for those cues, they often start screaming at us. Don't let it get that far. We encourage you to check in with your body regularly.

3. **Narrating your thoughts** is a fabulous technique that encourages you to become a curious observer. When you have a thought, literally narrate to yourself, "I am having the thought that . . ." *fill in the blank*. For example:
    - I am having the thought that my spouse is angry with me.
    - I am having the thought that it's a nice day outside today, and I should go do something.
    - I am having the thought that I need to empty the dishwasher.

As you narrate your thoughts, simply note them without judgment, saying, "Hmm, interesting" or "Huh." This puts you in the mode of a curious observer and allows you to evaluate the thoughts that your brain comes up with. Returning to the first example about your spouse being angry with you, simply having the thought doesn't mean he *is* angry with you. Where are the facts? You can also narrate what is going on with your brain. For example, you could say, "There goes the rumination monster revving up for a good old-fashioned brooding session." Or "There goes my anxiety brain churning my fears." Remind yourself that you are not your anxiety, depression, OCD, ADHD, or reigning national champion overthinker title. Not only does this increase your awareness, but it also separates your badass self from your brain and some of the crazy shit it creates.

4. **Arm yourself with ready-to-go mantras** to encourage awareness. Make them up yourself, or try one of these:
    - I have many thoughts and can choose the ones I agree with.
    - Thoughts are just habits.
    - I am not my thoughts.
    - My job is to observe my thoughts.
5. **Use Acronyms** to slow down, check in, and focus on your thoughts. Below are commonly used acronyms used in mindfulness practices that you may find helpful.
    - **STOP**—**S**top, **T**ake a breath, **O**bserve your experience, **P**roceed.
    - **RAIN**—**R**ecognize, **A**llow the experience to be there, **I**nvestigate with curiosity, and **N**urture with self-compassion. **COAL**—**C**uriosity, **O**penness, **A**cceptance, **L**ove.
6. **Thanking your mind** is another good tactic because thoughts are often products of the mind protecting us in some way. Pretend you're getting ready to give a presentation at work, and your mind spits out the thought, *I'm going to screw it up*. Your

brain, being the self-protecting guru that it is, is instilling fear and limitations to keep you from getting hurt or embarrassed. So, give your brain a little acknowledgment, something like *Thanks, mind, for having that thought and trying to protect me. I'll be just fine.* Then go kick some ass on your presentation.

✶ **It's Your Turn to Play, Learn, and Explore** ✶

The Bus Visualization

This imaginative and engaging visualization encourages awareness and separation from your thoughts. Remember, you are not your thoughts, and quite a few are complete BS!

- Pretend your brain is the driver of a bus. Your thoughts are the passengers. Picture your brain's adorable little bus driver's cap, vest, and entire outfit. Is your brain wearing sensible shoes or rocking some platforms?

- On your little bus trip of life, some of the passengers sit nicely and quietly. Other ones are kind of jerks, distracting you and calling out directions while you're trying to drive the damn bus.

- As the driver, you can choose how you respond to the passengers.

    ▸ You can ignore them, laugh at them, tell them to pipe down, or make them get off at the next stop.

    ▸ You can also just keep driving while they chatter away. Just notice them and half listen to their conversations while you turn up the radio with upbeat, positive messages playing (a.k.a. the mantra station).

    ▸ If you are feeling a bit spicy, you can give your thoughts the middle finger, wink, or blow them a kiss, letting them know you are not accepting any of their negativity!

GUIDE TO CREATING YOUR OWN MANTRAS

ARE YOU READY? It's time to get down, get funky, and create your own mantras! We know you will have fun collecting inspirational nuggets of wisdom and folding them into the healthy thoughts you create. The following questions integrate all the good stuff you'll need to consider when creating your personalized messages. Going through this process will help you realize that your perceptions *can* shift and there are healthier ways of thinking. In other words, change is possible! We've listed a few examples to give you ideas, and then there is a blank questionnaire so you can try it on your own.

Sample #1
What is the trigger or situation (who, what, where, when) and the thought or belief?
I have so much to do. I will never get it all done. I know that I tend to tie my self-worth with how much I get done. On the weekends, I need to clean the whole house, go grocery shopping, wash the clothes, change the sheets, mop the floors, cook food for the week; the list goes on.

Pay close attention to your emotions or feelings.

- Stress

- Dread

- Guilt

Challenge your thoughts and think about their origin.
I would like to focus on getting one thing done at a time and not freaking out if everything doesn't get done. I think I have these thoughts because I saw my mom doing everything growing up, and I want to be the same way.

But I am still valuable no matter how much I get done. I need to let myself enjoy life along the way. I'd like to take more mindful pauses in my life and move away from perfectionism.

Note some ways you can practice being aware of your body. This will lead to a more accurate acknowledgment of your thoughts and feelings.
- I will take deep breaths regularly, think about my posture, and do some stretching every hour for my neck.

Is there a visual image that would help you separate from your thoughts and feelings?
- Thinking of my thoughts as a river flowing.

Is there a song, quote, saying, or movie line that inspires you?
- "My List"—song by Toby Keith

- "I'm in a Hurry (and Don't Know Why)"—song by Alabama

- "Anxiety's like a rocking chair. It's something to do, but it doesn't get you very far." —Jodi Picoult

- "Fuck it, Dude, let's go bowling." —Walter in *The Big Lebowski*

Brainstorm healthy words or phrases to tell yourself when unwanted thoughts and feelings occur.
- I need to have "living" on my to-do list.
- Life is not about perfection.
- Anxiety doesn't get me very far.
- I'm not in a hurry.
- Let's go bowling.

Pick the phrase that resonates the most with you.

Your Mantra: Living is on my list!

Sample #2

This example is streamlined for those who like to keep it simple, and it's also for chart lovers! You know who you are . . .

Trigger or Situation	Emotions or Feelings	Automatic Thoughts	Body Sensations	Replacement Thought
My house is a mess and my husband invited people over after work today.	Embarrassment, panic, frustration, resentment, dread, anxiety	I suck at adulting! I can never keep the house clean. They are going to judge me.	My jaw is clenched, my chest is tight, and my stomach hurts.	I am doing the best I can. Our friends are coming to see us, not our house. **Mantra:** Just Do Your Best!

Your Turn!

What is the trigger or situation (who, what, where, when) and the thought or belief?

Pay close attention to your emotions or feelings.

Challenge your thoughts and think about their origin.

Note some ways you can practice being aware of your body. This will lead to a more accurate acknowledgment of your thoughts and feelings.

Is there a visual image that would help you separate from your thoughts and feelings?

Is there a song, quote, saying, or movie line that inspires you?

Brainstorm healthy words or phrases to tell yourself when unwanted thoughts and feelings occur.

Pick the phrase that resonates the most with you.

Your Mantra: _____

Trigger or Situation	Emotions or Feelings	Automatic Thoughts	Body Sensations	Replacement Thought
				<u>Mantra:</u>

PERSONALIZE, EXPAND, AND IMPLEMENT

MANTRAS ARE NOT a one-size-fits-all affair! For this reason, we have listed a smattering of alternate mantras for you to explore in part II at the end of each chapter. Naturally, we can all relate to mantras that promote a sense of well-being, but the wording, origin, and context of a mantra are deeply personal. It's surprisingly fun to discover cool phrases or simply make shit up. Mantra material is all over the place! Look for information and inspiration regarding your topic through different venues such as articles, songs, movies, books, the internet, quotes, cartoons, affirmations, or browsing sessions at your local library or bookstore. Use foul language in your mantra if necessary; it's therapeutic. If you like a quote but the exact wording doesn't work for you, keep changing it up until it is your own. Simply put, the phrase you want to go with is one that you will use and remember.

Whether you're creating your own mantra or using one out of this book, expand on the idea as much as possible. It will help attach more meaning to it. Having more meaning translates into more relatability and usefulness for you. When you repeat the mantra to yourself, all the stuff you've gathered in connection to the phrase will be brought into your mind. Years of psychological research reveals that the more leg work you put into any venture, the more personally and emotionally invested you'll be in the outcome. So do the leg work on your mantra; it's worth it!

When it comes to integrating mantras into your life, variety has proven to be a huge benefit. The famous phrase "Variety is the spice of life," by eighteenth-century poet William Cowper, applies to mantras too. There's also a lot of science behind this idea. Educators agree that when presenting a new concept, it's more effective to present the information through different modalities. This applies to integrating new information and material into your life as well. How you choose to incorporate your mantra into your life is based on personal preference and the type of change you wish to achieve. Here are some ideas to help you get started:

- **Obviously, we love sticky notes**! Even poster-sized sticky notes are available if you prefer a big one you can't miss. These visual cues help *stick* your mantra in your mind. They are simple but make a huge difference. First, they'll take over your mind, and then they'll take over the world! Bwahahaha!

- **Set aside a mindful focus time** and go over your mantra and all that it means to you. Take deep breaths and let the message flow through your mind, meditation style. Set reminders on your phone every hour or two to let you know it's mantra go-time.

- **Create a mantra playlist!** Jam out to songs that support your mantra while you're getting ready in the morning, on the way to work, cleaning the house, walking the dog, etc. Create a playlist that is ready to go when you need to hear a little mantra inspiration. Throughout this book, we have listed songs that support each mantra. Music is very individual, so just use the lists as a starting point to explore and create your own mantra playlist for every occasion.

- Start a **mantra accountability group!** Meet once a week or month to discuss your progress, support each other, and elaborate on your goals. You can even blend this with already existing groups such as book clubs, mom clubs, or hiking clubs. Of course, good snacks are a given for these meetings. There is a saying that supports this line of thinking: feed them, and they will come!

- **Journal and write about your mantra** in regard to the day's events. Use the **KISS principle** (keep it simple, stupid), or go to town and write a bunch of details with body sensations, thoughts, feelings, and images. Remember, there is no right or wrong way to journal. You can freestyle, brainstorm, outline, or doodle; you do you!

- **Create an affirmation** related to your mantra. Start the day off with your affirmation. "I" statements are empowering here. You can soften the language if you struggle to connect with your statement. For example, instead of saying, "I am at peace," you can go with, "I am open to the idea of letting peace in my life," or "I'm willing to start believing I can find peaceful moments."

- **Come forth, crafty and artistic people.** We know you're out there! Have you ever heard that art is therapeutic? That shit is real! Incorporate words relevant to your message into amazing art and jewelry projects. Make a talisman you can carry,

like a painted mantra rock. Scrapbook the hell out of your mantra, or create a vision board. Find a frame to put your mantra in if you'd like a more permanent visual cue. You can fancify it by blinging the crap out of a plain frame. Let go, be free, and experiment. Spend an hour at your local craft or dollar store, and you'll be swimming with ideas from simple to over-the-top.

- **Visual mantras** can be powerful tools to use in conjunction with your words. The good part is, no matter where you go, you can always take it with you in your mind. Learning to slow down and visualize your calming, motivating, or balancing mental picture can add a lot to your mantra. Think of a vacation spot or an everyday sight that goes with your new message. Include all the senses in your description whenever possible to increase the vivacity of your image.

The sky's the limit for integrating mantras into your life. Keep looking for fresh and fun ways to incorporate them into your scenery. The more cues around you, the more you strengthen your healthy thought muscles. And creating and cultivating your mantra collection will have more meaning to you. So, have fun and go a bit wild. Heck, go ahead and get crazy!

CLOSING

WE'RE ALL CREATURES of habit, especially when we feel stressed out, tired, overcommitted, or simply not at our best. In tough times, our brains will go to the most straightforward, accessible thought patterns. That, friends, is when those old, well-played, unhealthy, and dysfunctional thoughts resurface. Oh, and they are not alone because our thoughts also create those lovely, uncomfortable feelings we've been dodging. The overwhelming presence of these negative thoughts and feelings sets the stage for why and how we get stuck! But never fear; awareness plus redirection using mantras will help diffuse those thoughts. Just as your outlook evolved in bits and pieces over time, so do changes. We don't simply overhaul ourselves with a one-shot approach; it's a gradual process. Think baby steps because changes are made in specks, granules, smidgens, and occasional large chunks. Portia Nelson, the fabulous author and composer, talks about the slow process of change in the following poetic interlude, which she calls *My Autobiography in Five Short Chapters*:

I
I walk down the street.
There is a deep hole in the sidewalk.
I fall in.
I am lost . . . I am helpless. It isn't my fault.
It takes forever to find a way out.

II

I walk down the same street. There is a deep hole in the sidewalk.
I pretend I don't see it.
I fall in again.
I can't believe I am in the same place. But it still isn't my fault.
It still takes a long time to get out.

III

I walk down the same street.
There is a deep hole in the sidewalk.
I see it there.
I still fall in. It's a habit.
My eyes are open. I know where I am. It is my fault.
I get out immediately.

IV

I walk down the same street.
There is a deep hole in the sidewalk.
I walk around it.

V

I walk down a different street.

Portia nailed it. Changing destructive beliefs and behaviors doesn't happen all at once. Be patient. It takes time. Expect to mess up from time to time, especially during times of stress. It's all a part of the process. We promise, with a little *stick-to-itiveness*, change can and will happen!

We believe in you, and we know you will kick ass on this journey and create some downright badass mantras of your own. We'd love to hear from you! Let us know the fabulous messages and implementation ideas you come up with at www.stickynotemantras.com, and we will share them with other Sticky Note Mantras aficionados.

BETH AND HELENE'S PERSONAL MANTRA STORIES

* Helene *

MY STORY WITH mantras starts with a knock-down, drag-out fight with obsessive compulsive disorder (OCD) from the time I was a child. Let me tell you, this shit is no joke. Fears constantly hijacked my brain. Fears that something terrible would happen, fear of losing my connections with others, fears of being misunderstood, and fears of not being enough. These thoughts *felt* life-threatening to me. Sweaty hands, increased heart rate, and shallow breathing commenced every time the cycle began, even though they were just . . . thoughts. While there was no real emergency, it felt like a gun was pointed straight between my eyes. I would perform rituals until it "felt right," which never happened, to keep my thoughts from materializing. And then there was the counting. I counted a certain number of times in rapid succession while involved in said rituals. My number was four for a long time. I could count sixty-four sets of four so fast, it was ridiculous. This whole process of fuckery consumed my every waking moment. Let me give you a glance into my past, a typical dinner scenario in my high school years.

Sitting at the kitchen table, I glance up at the round straw basket hanging on the wall for the umpteenth time. I roll my neck in a circle, flex one wrist, then the other, blink, and swallow. Goddamn it. That didn't feel right. I have to do the whole thing again. I start to count again in my mind at a rapid pace: one, two, three, four, one, two, three, four, one, two, three, four, one, two, three, four. That's four sets of four. At this point, I glance up at the basket, making sure I see the edges. Then I repeat the whole sequence (I'm on the second time through). I do it again (third time). And again. Okay, I've done four sets of four, four times. As I stare at the basket for the last time, I roll my neck around three hundred and sixty degrees, flex one wrist immediately after the other, blink, and swallow. Shit. That didn't feel right either. Flames of doubt and anxiety continue to eat away at me. Something bad is going to happen. My mom encourages me to eat my dinner, telling me everyone else is already almost finished. I nod my head and try to take a deep breath. My throat is caving in, and spit keeps foaming up in my mouth. I pause and gaze up at the plastic sheets of tiny white squares covering the fluorescent lighting above me. Forty-eight squares in each row, to be exact. I shut my eyes and can still see the outline of the lights. It's a nice diversion, but I know what awaits me. I start the counting sequence over in my head.

That stupid straw basket above the kitchen table is forever imprinted in my mind. Actually, I stared at specific objects in each room of our house while doing counting sequences. The cherry wood clock in the family room, the outline of the window in my bedroom, and the brown rod holding up the pale-blue drapes in my parent's room are still very clear to me. I had objects in each one of my classrooms too. I don't remember when I started doing these things, nor do I remember a time when I didn't do them. I certainly never enjoyed any of this stuff. In fact, I loathed it. It stole all my time and energy, not to mention my sanity. Knowing that these behaviors made no sense whatsoever just added to my frustration. Any way you look at it, the cycle was a lose-lose situation. Anxiety would consume me if I didn't engage in the rituals, and they were never good enough when I did. It was the ultimate damned if you do damned if you don't situation. So, I got used to living life with an underlying level of tension and anxiety. Sometimes, my fears were ambiguous, just a heavy sense of doom, and other times, they were explicitly played out in my mind. They shifted throughout the years, depending on my experiences and stage in life. Someone I loved getting hurt was a big theme. Another big one was someone misunderstanding me or no longer loving me. Occasionally, things that absolutely disgusted me popped into my mind. If I saw something that could be used as a weapon, I'd obsess that I'd pick it up and use it to hurt someone. Inappropriate sexual images floated around in my head. Blasphemous phrases. You name it, I thought of it.

I had so many rituals, I can't even remember them all. Rolling my neck, breathing in a certain way, turning things on and off, scratching my head, taking caps to bottles on and off, saying certain things over and over, and flexing my wrists are just a few that come to mind. Before bed, I endlessly adjusted my buttocks, trying to end on the elusive "good" thought. That was a particularly miserable and uncomfortable one. Certain words had connotations, and I couldn't end sentences with them. Looking in a mirror was linked with the thought that I'd become vain. I had to draw an invisible line with my feet so my loved ones were on the correct side, or something bad would happen. My brother sleeping in the bedroom down the hall screwed up everything line-wise. I remember thinking, *I wonder if he'd switch bedrooms with me?* Writing was difficult because each letter had a bad thought linked to it, so I spent a lot of time rewriting and erasing. Taking notes in high school was painful, to say the least. Speaking of high school, I got up at the crack of dawn because it took me so long to get ready with my rituals. In college, I vividly remember a terrible episode, trying to put a piece of paper in a folder. I was up the whole damn night and ended up stabbing a pencil into my thigh out of sheer desperation and mental exhaustion.

I finally learned about OCD from a book and then saw a video with examples of people's struggles. It was such a *holy shit* moment for me. I wanted to scream, "*You mean other people have trouble folding a towel just one time too?*" All that time, I just thought I was nuts. Today, it's so much more out in the open, visible in movies and the media, but back then, uh-uh. It helped to know I wasn't alone. However, having

OCD is not something I usually shared with people. I was ashamed and felt like such a weirdo for doing these bizarre things and being unable to let things go. I started getting some help and learned about my brain and its false messages. I remember a psychiatrist explaining it by drawing a triangle on a piece of paper and saying most people's thoughts bounce to each point and then move on. My thoughts, on the other hand, were getting stuck in the triangle and never making an exit. I became a little more open about what was happening with those closest to me since I had a name for my problem. My mom was a huge source of comfort and collaboration.

I came to find out she had these problems as well. So did many other people in our family. Genetics is real! Mom and I started making up mantras to interrupt my thought process. The one that really worked for me was, "That's a brain glitch. I don't have to pay attention to that." I found the most amazing book about OCD called *Brain Lock* by Jeffrey M. Schwartz. That thing was like my Bible, and it described OCD flawlessly. His method for addressing OCD involved recognizing your OCD thought, reattributing it (calling it bullshit), and then refocusing your attention. He said you could rewire your brain by doing this. . . . I realized that was what I was doing with my mantras! They honestly saved my sanity. By continually interrupting thoughts and replacing them, I created new neural pathways and rewired my fucked-up brain. I'm not saying it was easy or I won the battle every time. But it's been many, many years, and I can honestly say OCD doesn't haunt me today. Sure, I have tendencies when I'm stressed, and my mind wants to return to the old patterns. But it is nothing compared to what it used to be.

So, there you have it—my mantra story. And mantras live on in my life today. I use them for all kinds of topics, such as perfectionism, balance, acceptance, encouragement, and validation. I met Beth in graduate school in 1998, and we clicked immediately. We discovered that we both used mantras personally and in our work as educators and counselors. The mantras Beth introduced me to, or we created together, have enriched my life more than I can say. Beth is one of the most authentic, compassionate, and fucking hilarious people I know. We've been collaborating about mantras for years now, refining the process. The rest is history!

✳ Beth ✳

My parents did not plan on having a fourth child, but God or the universe either loves irony or has a great sense of humor. Case in point: when I was born, I entered this world holding the very object that was supposed to prevent my existence: a copper IUD. I was pushed out into the world, gripping it tightly in my little fist, waving it around, boldly flaunting that divine sense of humor. Dr. Simon, our family physician, was kind enough to offer it to my mom for my baby scrapbook. But, to my complete and utter disappointment, she declined. A fourth child was not really in the family plan for my parents, but this tracks well with my life story. *Scattered and Unplanned* should be the name of my autobiography because, on many levels, my life has been a wild ride of unplanned surprises and nebulous feelings of not belonging.

My parents never made me feel like I was unwanted. But don't worry, my sisters didn't hesitate to remind me that I was not a part of the initial family plan. However, I believe I am a fantastic reminder of life's charming surprises. My feelings of not belonging stem more from the irrefutable fact that I am an introvert. In most social situations, I feel like I am standing outside, looking in. It's like social interactions are a classic board game, and I am the extra piece on the sidelines, observing but never actually in the game. Whenever I find myself in the unfortunate position of attending a social event, my husband and I joke that having a glass of wine or a beer is me having a "glass of extrovert."

I was blissfully unaware of my introverted tendencies in elementary school, but I had other challenges thrown my way. At the time, ADHD was not really on very many educators' radars, especially not for girls. But the clues that I have ADHD were clearly written in most of my teachers' grade report comments. Adjectives teachers often used to describe my behavior at school were forgetful, fidgety, messy, disorganized, unfocused, and chatty. Growing up, I never felt confident or successful in the classroom. I walked around every day with this giant knot of fear or anxiousness, sitting squarely in the pit of my stomach. This knot was made up of a mishmash of thoughts about being different, being dumb, or just falling short in some way. I realize now that we all have our gifts and talents. Mine just didn't happen to fall anywhere near the vicinity of elementary school. I did have other unidentified learning differences besides ADHD, like mild dyslexia and dysgraphia. Those little gifts of genetics came with the added bonus of shame and more anxiety. I did not learn about these differences until I was well into my forties, but they left a massive scar on my psyche. I frequently grappled with my self-concept, which liked to remind me that something was clearly wrong with me. I'm sure that was a big part of that giant knot I carried around in my stomach for over forty-five years.

Socially, things weren't easy for me. I didn't really like myself, so I figured neither would my peers. I started to observe others and did my best to act like them. *Fake it until you make it* is a very polite way to describe what I was attempting to do. Psychologists came up with the term *masking* to describe people like me who put on a social facade to fit in or appear to be just like everybody else. Let me tell you, masking was and still is exhausting.

Like so many adolescents, I lost my sense of self somewhere in that period. I invested all my time and energy into trying to be more of someone else and less of me. *More is better* seemed like a sound strategy in my adolescent brain. I began talking too much. I made too many jokes. I was often too loud and outrageous. I clearly did not understand the concept of moderation or the art of being subtle. In my mind, if something seemed good and made me feel accepted, then more was better.

Except it wasn't, and eventually, my faking and excessiveness backfired. My masking and efforts to be extroverted and fit in made me miserable. So, I would retreat to my bed and escape by reading books. Reading about the growing pains and tween awkwardness that littered Scholastic Book fairs was grounding for me. It gave me a respite from adolescent drama, got me out of my own head, and redirected my downward spirals.

In the early 1980s, my family and I spent a long summer in the Dominican Republic. This was *not* the popular tropical vacation destination it is today. It was a third-world country with shady political shenanigans keeping its economy on the struggle bus. So, when I was chilling in the DR, exploring or playing tourist was not an option. We were mostly on lockdown inside our hotel resort, with only three channels of television, all in Spanish. However, my sisters and I brought several books we read numerous times. It was a very relaxing time. I didn't have to labor through reading aloud the words with the judgment of teachers or snickers of my classmates when my pronunciation of words went awry. I didn't have to rush through the stories and finish when it looked and sounded like everyone else was finished. Those weeks cooped up in a hotel room, reading at my leisure, were truly a gift. It allowed me to remove my feelings of fear and shame away from the act of reading and reassociate books with positive feelings. To this day, reading is associated with feelings of peace, awe, and wonderment, no matter how good or bad the book might be.

The books I read growing up laid the groundwork for how and why mantras became important to me. I read every book by James Harriet, John Steinbeck, and Judy Bloom. I read my mom's celebrity books like *Elvis and Me,* and I relished my dad's Clive Cussler books and the wild adventures of Dirk Pitt. These books kept me interested in learning and tethered to my family and authentic self. They gave me a respite from my life. At some point, I started to underline or pull quotes that inspired me or tugged on my emotions. Being the disorganized ADHD kid that I was, these quotes were everywhere! Napkins, notebooks, scrap paper, arms, shoes, bags, whatever was handy when I got inspired. The author's words seemed to elicit something good and wise in my brain. I loved these nuggets of wisdom and poetry, and I wanted to keep them close by. These quotes became my guideposts, my directions for adolescence, and they gave me much-needed solace and direction.

I was a tween in the 1980s, and popular media and magazines influenced my life. In 1988, when Nike released its famous *Just Do It* media campaign, I was awestruck! My ADHD-muddled, procrastinating brain had and still has a mental to-do list several pages long. I started seeing *Just Do It* everywhere, which was a game-changer. I wrote *Just Do It* all over my school notebooks. *Just Do It* served as my cue to put my fears and doubts aside and work. *Just Do It* evolved into "rip the Band-Aid," a.k.a. *do that shit you don't want to do now*! It flat-out worked for me. *Just Do It* got me unstuck, moving forward, and out of my negative thought cycles. My inner critic was always running amok, and these cues gave me the wherewithal to override my harsh inner voice. I did not know I was utilizing mantras until I met Helene.

As she mentioned, we met in grad school and just hit it off. I remember pulling out my phone during a class break and showing her several pictures of my dogs because I am a socially awkward oversharer. Somewhere in our conversations, she told me about mantras, which was an aha moment for me. Just like learning about ADHD, the puzzle pieces started to fit. I was like, *yes!* Mother-fucking mantras; that's exactly what I had been using all this time!

Fast-forward twenty-plus years, and here we are writing all kinds of terrific shit about using mantras as a strategy. I want to stress that mantras are not a cure-all, but peeps, if you put in the effort, mantras shift your thinking bit by bit. Be curious. Be inspired. Fail and learn! Do the work. It's remarkable how the subtle shifts add up to make a big difference!

PART II:
Mantras for Everyday Obstacles

Rainy Day Mantras
for When Shit Goes Sideways

OUR MINDS ARE a lot like the weather in the sky. Sometimes, there are clear and sunny days. Other times, dark clouds roll in and put a damper on everything. Rainy day mantras are a much-needed umbrella for the storms we all experience. In this weather, encouragement from our inner selves is often scarce. Ironically, it's when they're most needed. Our inner critic goes on a roll and hits us with a one-two punch when we're already down, saying things like, *You suck. You can't do anything right. What is wrong with you? Why are you this way? Look how much better that person is doing than you. Why can't you do more, be more?* and on and on. While our inner critics are trying to protect us, it is not helpful! Never fear; rainy day mantras are here to redirect our thoughts and quiet down that mean-spirited asswipe of an inner bully! What follows are mantras we have found effective on those rainy days. They'll help shut down the autopilot so you can fly your own plane in clear skies again.

"Imperfection is beauty, madness is genius, and it's better to be absolutely ridiculous than absolutely boring."

—MARILYN MONROE

THE EXPECTATION THAT everything must be perfect is plain silly. Yet, many of us feel perfection is the gold standard. Pursuing "perfect" leads to a word we all know: perfectionism. Perfectionism is linked with all kinds of mental health challenges, such as depression and anxiety. It should be quite simple: we are fallible human beings, meaning we are all less than perfect. However, our minds frequently insist that nothing is ever good enough. Finding ways to accept and embrace imperfection leads to positive things like more life satisfaction, relaxation, and happiness. Sara Evans beautifully illustrates this in her song "Perfect," the ultimate theme song for this mantra! While Sara's focus is on love, the message can be generalized to all sorts of situations. She sings, "Don't you know that all the fairy tales tell a lie. Real love and real life doesn't have to be perfect." Perfection is a notion in our mind that we *can* start to look at differently. It's the imperfections that bring variety, novelty, and beauty into our lives.

Today, it seems many expectations are so high that there's no way we could ever be satisfied. This idea extends from expectations in our relationships to those involving our well-being, jobs, accomplishments, possessions, family, and more. Our internal voice, influenced by mass media, misguidedly tells us we must have more, be more, and do more to be enough. It also tells us we need approval and acceptance from others instead of focusing on improvement and growth. So, if you're asking yourself how to improve, you're on the right track. If you're asking yourself what other people will think, then it sounds like perfectionism is making an appearance. Squash it with this mantra.

> **Repeat while taking a deep cleansing breath:**
> *Imperfection is Beauty.*

Another aspect of perfectionism involves not wanting to take risks or try new things for fear that our best will not be good enough. With this attitude, we may as well never do anything, crawl under a rock, and stay there because *life inherently comes with imperfection.* Doing your best is all you can ask of yourself, and your best will look different on different days. Remembering this simple fact relieves a lot of stress and encourages us to relax. Being in a relaxed state promotes a more positive performance and outcome in any task. This message comes through loud and clear in this shortened excerpt from Don Miguel Ruiz's phenomenal book *The Four Agreements*:

> Under any circumstance, always do your best, no more and no less. But keep in mind that your best is never going to be the same from one moment to the next. Everything is alive and changing all the time, so your best will sometimes be high quality, and other times it will not be as good. . . . In your everyday moods, your best can change from one moment to another, from one hour to the next, from one day to another. Your best will also change over time, but

keep doing your best —no more and no less than your best. If you try too hard and do more than your best, you will spend more energy than is needed and in the end your best will not be enough. When you overdo, you deplete your body and go against yourself and it will take longer to accomplish your goal.

Ruiz's elegant message of simply doing your best encourages us to accept the reality that some days we will achieve more than others. There are days and times to back off and be conscious not to do *more* than your best. Otherwise, you'll be in the danger zone of becoming unnecessarily stressed out, overdoing it, and missing the whole point of what you were trying to accomplish in the first place. On the other hand, we're sure there have been times you have done a half-hearted job and been sorry about it later. We've all been there. The message remains: *just do your best*. No more, no less! Balance is the keyword and an important concept that easily becomes out of sync if we are not pausing and practicing awareness.

✴ Helene ✴

THERE SHOULD BE a whole organization for us perfectionists where we can gather and work through our stuff together. "Hi, my name is Helene, and I'm a perfectionist. Oh, shit, let me start over. That didn't sound right." Only another perfectionist understands those unrealistic expectations and fears of negative evaluations from themselves and others. It's a self-destructive cycle. I've found focusing on doing everything just right encourages me to believe I'm not good enough. This gets magnified by a lovely little thing called rumination. Rumination of how others see me, how I said or did things, and whether I should have done things differently. I now realize that I achieve less due to perfectionism because it contributes to my already stressful days and wastes my time and energy. So, having a mantra at the ready is huge for me. It switches off my autopilot and shifts the outlandish perfectionist narratives I tell myself. When I view imperfection as a fact of life and part of our world's beauty, I start to accept myself, relax, and enjoy life more. The messages we tell ourselves are so powerful! I love how Marisa Peer, British therapist and author, talks about imperfection and vulnerability: "We like people who are a little flawed, a little vulnerable, because it allows us to be a little flawed, a little vulnerable. Vulnerability does not equal weakness. It equals courage. The imperfections make you human, so stop trying to be perfect and love your flaws."

It's true. It's pretty hard to like someone who seems perfect, right? I don't know about you, but I feel much better when I realize even people who appear to be perfect on the outside have vulnerabilities. We all just have different ones. I'm not quite at the point of *loving* my flaws like Marissa suggests, but I realize they're a part of life, and we all have them. I've found being authentic and vulnerable leads to deeper connections with others. If you're a fellow perfectionist, I hope this mantra takes the winds out of your perfectionism's sails.

※ Beth ※

TRADITIONAL JAPANESE CULTURE has a philosophy called *kintsugi* that encourages us to value imperfection. I was introduced to this concept in the hospital following a severe car accident. I was laying in my bed contemplating my brokenness, feeling my collapsed lung, torn tendons, and basic fucked-up-ness. In those moments, I wholeheartedly believed I was a broken person. I had no idea how to process this new version of myself.

One day, a kind, soulful volunteer came to my room and asked if he could talk with me. At the time, I was still on some pretty high doses of Dilaudid, a synthetic morphine that is about eight times stronger than your typical morphine. So, basically flying high and ready for anything, I invited him to sit by my bed. He introduced himself as a pay-it-forward person who had also been in a life-altering accident. He explained that he periodically returned to the hospital to

Kintsugi
Beth's
Japanese Bowl

Car Accident • Dyslexia • Elementary School • ADHD • Parents Fighting • College Softball

offer busted-up people like me hope. And it worked. He did bring me hope. That little four-letter word is much needed when you are stuck in a hospital bed, staring down the long road of recovery. My memory of the entire conversation is a bit hazy, but I do remember him telling me in his quiet, gentle voice about the Japanese art of *kintsugi*.

Kintsugi is an art form that creates beauty out of imperfection. It takes broken pottery and mends them into beautiful works of art by filling in the cracks with delicate, intricate patterns of gold. And guess what? The beauty truly lies in the imperfection. He played this song by Peter Mayer called "Japanese Bowls." I remember listening to the words:

> *I'm like one of those Japanese Bowls*
> *That were made long ago*
> *I have some cracks in me*
> *They have been filled with gold*
> *That's what they used back then*
> *When they had a bowl to mend*
> *It did not hide the cracks*
> *It made them shine instead*
> *So now every old scar shows*
> *from every time I broke*

My Dilaudid-flooded self was, of course, crying and thanking him. I found and purchased the song, which started reframing how I viewed my injuries. Today, I have a smattering of scars all over my body from this accident. I don't try to hide them, and I do not feel shame about them when my husband sees my body. Although my cracks are only filled with dull metals like titanium and surgical steel and not gold, I now only see their beauty. I survived. I can walk. I can enjoy yoga and walking my dogs. My scars and imperfections are not ugly to me. They are just a part of my story and only a small part of who I am today.

> **Take a deep breath and repeat:**
> *Imperfection is a part of being human.*

Albert Einstein said, "Anyone who has never made a mistake hasn't tried anything new." He's right, and there's just no getting around it. Mistakes can, will, and do happen. We make the wrong choices, are pressured into situations that test our values, and sometimes just seriously screw things up. When we view mistakes as natural and normal, we're more likely to use them as a jumping place towards growth. Dr. Jane Nelson, a psychologist, wrote about this very thing. "You are not supposed to be perfect. If you were, what would you have to learn? *Understanding* that you are not supposed to be perfect can help you relax and lovingly accept your imperfections as wonderful opportunities to learn—and to enjoy the process."

Let's face it, if you were perfect and never made any mistakes, you would not only be annoying and delusional but also not learn the valuable lessons needed to live a safe, happy, and healthy life. To begin with, any choice, mistake or not, comes with consequences. Natural consequences are the logical effects of our choices. These consequences may be beneficial, such as, "I chose to speak to our new neighbor, and now I have a new friend," or harmful, such as, "I chose to stay up and watch the late-night movie, and now I'm tired and can't concentrate." These types of natural consequences serve an important purpose. They keep us from repeating unhealthy choices. There is an old saying, "Fool me once, shame on you. Fool me twice, shame on me." This saying is a catchy way of reminding us that mistakes are educational, and we should take the time to heed the lesson. They provide us with material to educate our minds and help us make better life choices. After all, mistakes are about learning, growing, and building a source of information. They create a wealth of knowledge to draw on when making tough choices.

Another example is, "Every time I date an aggressive man, I end up being controlled and lost in the relationship. I will make a change. I will seek out relationships that make me feel safe and comfortable." So, embrace your mistakes and let yourself experience the feelings related to them. Then, analyze them for their lessons. There is always a lesson to be found. Sometimes, it is a small lesson, such as, "Don't touch a hot stove," or sometimes, a big one, such as, "That DUI cost me dearly."

Most of us find it difficult to move on from mistakes. Our inner critic pops up with negative self-talk. *What was I thinking? How could I be so stupid? Why didn't I think that through a little more?* Sometimes, we replay memories with the outcome we wished had happened. However, those of us who ruminate only hold ourselves back. Research shows that athletes who move on quickly following a mistake consistently outperform mistake dwellers in competitions across the sports spectrum. So, we must acknowledge our mistakes and the feelings they produce to *move forward* and reach our full potential.

Try pulling out a quote to help you when you are worried about failure. This one by Louisa May Alcott is one of our favorites. "I am not afraid of storms, for I am learning how to sail my ship." Another fantastic alternate mantra is *I've had my moments,* based on a song entitled "Moments" by Emerson Drive. "Moments" is about a man who is standing next to a bridge and contemplating ending his life. A homeless person who is hanging around realizes what is going on and talks to him. Both men feel ashamed of where they are in their lives—one man thinking of committing suicide and the other man without a home. They each share times when they were proud of themselves, saying,

> "I've had my moments, days in the sun
> Moments I was second to none
> Moments when I knew I did what I
> thought I couldn't do . . .
> Lookin' at me now you might not know it
> But I've had my moments."

In the end, the homeless man has another moment to be proud of; he saves the other guy's life by talking to him. *Hang on to those beautiful and empowering moments, not onto your mistakes.* Go ahead and let those fuckers go! Put this song on your playlist if it resonates with you, and let it remind you of all your shining moments.

✷ It's Your Turn to Play, Explore, and Learn ✷

<u>Identifying Your Trends</u>

Most of us have themes associated with our perfectionism. We've listed some questions below to help you become aware of your trends. After you are aware of what's going on, you can make a conscious choice to give it the finger and refocus on an empowering thought.

- In what areas of your life does perfectionism arise? Consider things like appearance, being liked by others, getting shit done around the house, wanting to be flawless at work or school, and feeling pressured to be in sync with your relationships at all times.

- What are some automatic thoughts you tell yourself? Do you have any all-or-nothing thinking going on in these areas?

- Brainstorm some balanced, flexible, and healthy thoughts to challenge your current patterns. A chart is an excellent way to visualize the different areas in your life. Fill in whatever topics you'd like to address.

Identify Your Trends

Topic	Activity	Belief	Balanced Thought
Work	Meeting with clients	If I am not perfect, I am not providing good care.	I am forever learning & provide the best care I can.
Relationships	Connecting with others	I want everyone to like me all of the time.	If I connect with others, YAY! If not, that's OK.
Around the House	Cleaning	The house needs to be clean at all times before I can relax.	Some days I will spend time cleaning and others I will not.
Appearance	Getting ready	If I look good, I am more worthy of love.	My beauty is internal.

The Why Exercise

It's good to dive deeper and determine where your beliefs come from. Knowing the *why* will make it easier to challenge and reshape your thoughts. Next to each scenario you listed in the chart above, make a new column that asks why. Why do you think you have this belief? Is the thought doing anything for you now? Researchers have developed three categories of perfectionism:

- **Self-Oriented**—demanding perfection of yourself.

- **Other Oriented**—demanding perfectionism from others.

- **Socially Prescribed**—when you feel pressure from others and societal cues to be perfect.

Label your perfectionistic beliefs into one of the three categories.

Visualize a Perfect World

Close your eyes and take a deep breath. Now, imagine a perfect world where mistakes don't exist. What's it like in the scenario you are visualizing? Think of a few sentences to describe it, then read on!

In our visits to a perfect world, we've noticed it kind of sucks. There's no sense of accomplishment in overcoming difficulties, no connections with others over our humanness, and humor is lacking. *Setbacks are part of the process* is a fabulous alternative mantra to increase our awareness that mistakes are a given. This phrase encourages us to *fail happily*, learn from it, and move on. Embrace mistakes as learning opportunities and growth instead of avoiding them and considering them to be evidence of inferiority. Happily acknowledge a few mistakes today!

✴ Inspirational Quotes that Support This Mantra ✴

- "I am not afraid of storms, for I am learning how to sail my ship."
  —Louisa May Alcott

- "The essence of being human is that one does not seek perfection."
  —George Orwell

- "Imperfection is the new perfection."
  —Hina Khan

- "Perfection is the willingness to be imperfect."
  —Lao Tzu

- "When perfectionism is driving us, shame is riding shotgun and fear is that annoying backseat driver!"
  —Brené Brown.

✴ Alternate Mantra Ideas for This Topic ✴

- I'm forever a work in progress.

- Setbacks are part of the process.
- I aim for growth, not perfection.
- I may not be perfect, but parts of me are pretty fabulous.
- I've had my moments.

✳ **Songs to Add to Your Imperfection Mantra Playlist** ✳

- "Just the Way"
    by Parmalee and Blanco Brown

- "Perfect"
    by Sara Evans

- "Free"
    by Anya Marina, feat Jewel and Tristan Prettyman

- "Bruises"
    by Train and Ashley Monroe

- "Moments"
    by Emerson Drive

✳ **Further Reading** ✳

- *Overcoming Perfectionism: The Key to a Balanced Recovery*
    by Ann W. Smith

- *The Four Agreements: A Practical Guide to Personal Freedom*
    by Don Miguel Ruiz

- *The Gifts of Imperfection: Let Go of Who You Think You're Supposed to Be and Embrace Who You Are*
    by Dr. Brené Brown

- *When Perfect Isn't Good Enough: Strategies for Coping with Perfectionism*
    by Dr. Martin M. Antony & Richard P. Swinson

"The magic is inside you. There ain't no crystal ball."

—Dolly Parton

THE POWER BEHIND this mantra is its simplicity. The word *believe* conjures up encouragement, empowerment, and trust in yourself. *Believe* cues your mind into remembering that you are valuable and deserving. It reminds you to look first and foremost to yourself for validation and self-compassion. Work on separating yourself from your achievements and accomplishments because you've always been far more important than the Wins you have logged. Believe in the power of you, no matter how much you've achieved or utterly failed.

It's fair to note that we all naturally look outside ourselves for others to validate us and tell us we are okay. Looking outside ourselves is perfectly natural and goes with the whole *being human* thing. However, if we place our self-worth *entirely* into the hands of others, we're setting the stage for an emotional roller-coaster ride. The renowned psychotherapist Fritz Perls said, "Our dependency makes slaves out of us, especially if this dependency is a dependency of our self-esteem. If you need encouragement, praise, pats on the back from everyone, then you make everyone your judge." Amen to that, Fritzy! People pleasers constantly ask themselves questions like *Does she like me? Does he like me? Do they like what I did?* When they feel the answer is affirmative, their brains give them a reinforcing shot of dopamine, and they feel fabulous. On the other hand, feeling the opposite way can send them into an anxiety attack or depressive episode. Yes, feeling everyone has to like you is a recipe for disappointment. Dita Von Tesse, the sexy, sultry, burlesque dancer, said it best: "You can be the ripest, juiciest peach in the world, and there's still going to be somebody who hates peaches."

It's true; you can be fantastic, funny, witty, charming, and gorgeous, and some people out there will not get you or like you. The irony is it's not even about you; it's all about them, about their own internal stuff. Have you ever heard the phrase *90 percent of what people say and do is about them, not you*? That's the idea here. People are simply acting on their perception of reality, which is colored by their own experiences, not so much on how great or not-so-great you are. So, work hard at being okay with not clicking with everyone. Reducing or eliminating our need for acceptance from others is freeing and oh-so worthwhile. The word *believe* encourages us to look first and foremost to ourselves for approval. *Am I proud of my choices? Am I okay with what I just finished? Am I proud of my actions? What is my opinion of my work? Did I give this my all? Do I think I am a caring person?* These internal questions prompt you to believe in your worth, opinions, and perspectives. It's like saying, "I will look to myself first for feedback, and then I can request or accept the feedback of others."

Once you start doing this, a fear of what others think will be replaced with a stronger belief in yourself. In the words of Renaissance writer Thomas à Kempis, "Great tranquility of heart is his who cares for neither praise nor blame." So, whether someone praises you for a job well done or conversely criticizes you, it's a similar situation. If *you* feel it was a job well done, that's what matters. Another way to put this is "praise and blame are all the same." Richard Carlson made up this catchy phrase in his book *Don't Sweat the Small Stuff (and it's All Small Stuff)*. It's a great reminder that putting too much value on what others think is not healthy. Let's be honest here—approval feels a hell of a lot better than disapproval. We all crave acceptance and praise. But the reality is, if you base all your happiness on the approval and opinion of others, you're setting yourself up for suffering. It leads to feeling less than and triggers shame when you don't get the approval you seek. *Believing* in your own opinions and feelings will lead you toward emotional freedom.

> **Repeat while taking a deep breath:**
> *I believe in myself, my values, and my opinions.*

As Beth mentioned in her personal story, the whole process of conforming and transforming yourself to please others is also known as masking, which is *exhausting*. The actor and comedian Jim Carrey, who openly shared his struggles with mental health, summed up the toll of masking perfectly. "Depression is your body saying fuck you, I don't want to be this character anymore. I don't want to hold this avatar that you have created in a world that's too much for me." Most of us know intuitively when our inside does not match our outside. We feel uncomfortable and often feel shame. This mismatch ultimately takes a toll on our energy, physical health, and souls. When we tell ourselves that who we are is not good enough or we must be someone else, it feels shitty. It's a Band-Aid fix, taking *faking it till you make it* too far. The first step in addressing this mismatch between the authentic self and the facade is *awareness*.

We are all social creatures with an innate need for emotional connections and belonging. And that's a very good thing! It's what makes us wonderful parents, partners, and friends. *But*, if we try to belong and connect by changing who we are to fit in, we are spinning our wheels because it is counterproductive. It interferes with our self-preservation, autonomy, and authentic sense of self. We've all been there, especially in our younger years, thinking, *I'll be anything you want me to be—just as long as you accept me and I belong!* However, real belonging happens when you accept your imperfect self. It happens when you are brave enough to put yourself out there and attract your tribe. Your tribe makes you feel good about your authentic self. However, if we base our connections and belonging on our fears (of not being enough, being unloved, being alone, or abandonment), that's when we turn away from our authentic selves. Author Sue Patton Thoele calls this phenomenon emotional dependence:

> *Before I ever heard the term 'emotional dependence,' I knew that, in some mysterious way, I turned my life over to other people. It didn't really matter who they were—my parents, husband, kids, coworkers. If they were happy with me, then I could be happy. If they approved of me, then I felt worthwhile. . . . Since I wasn't a mind reader, no matter what form I pretzeled myself into, I wasn't able to please everyone all of the time. But I tried. That's emotional dependence!*

We turn our self-worth over repeatedly to feel wanted, complete, and enough. *Believe* you are already enough with all your imperfections. It does not matter what stage you are at or how many connections you have. It does not matter how much you have done and whether you have the approval of others or not. What matters most is that you believe in you!

Believing can also mean fully expressing yourself. Minister, scholar, and social activist Dr. Benjamin E. Mays said, "Every person is born into the world to do something unique and something distinctive, and if he or she does not do it, it will never be done." We all play an important role in this life that no one else can. Once we get to know our true selves, we shouldn't be timid or shy. We must all express fully and freely who we authentically are. Think about all the times you have been encouraged or inspired by other people: reading a book, listening to a song, watching a great movie, looking at art, smiling at the kindness of a stranger . . . the list goes on. Most of the time, people will never know the full impact they have on others. Another favorite quote with this message comes from the famous American choreographer Martha Graham: "There is a vitality, a life force, an energy, a quickening, that is translated through you into action, and because there is only one of you in all of time, this expression is unique. And if you block it, it will never exist through any other medium and it will be lost." Individuals bring beauty, passion, and peace into the world through their expressions, directly or indirectly. In this way, we all need each other because we all enrich one another's lives. Believe in being who you are meant to be. Remember, there is only one of you out there.

> **Repeat while taking a deep breath,**
> *I believe . . . in my true, authentic, unique self.*

Many people go through periods in their lives when they don't accept or like the person they are. Introverts wish they could be more like extroverts, or those people who are serious by nature want to be more lighthearted and comedic. But self-acceptance of our true character, natural abilities, and temperament encourages inner peace. When we go against these, we set ourselves up for frustration. So, explore who you are, learn about yourself, know yourself inside and out, and then *believe*. Accepting and being yourself will bring you more peace of mind than you can imagine. This may take some exploring because there's an overload of input telling us who and what we should be. Family expectations, peer influences, the ever-present media, and motherfucking social media (it deserves this title because it tells us what we need, how we should act or dress, and to compare our lives to others) all influence our self-concept because we want to fit in with our community. They are the "nurture" in the whole nature versus nurture debate. Although these powerful influences can confuse our true identity, it doesn't mean we still can't be ourselves. Think of it this way: being your true self is comforting and calming. Conversely, going against your true self drains your physical and emotional energy. Being aware of our motivations for choices and behaviors is the key to discovering our authentic selves. Exploring our values, accepting our flaws in all their glory, and embracing our innate gifts are all a part of our lifelong journey. Do your best to live authentically and remember to always be kind to yourself along the way. As Kermit the frog so sagely put it, "It isn't easy being green."

✳ It's Your Turn to Play, Explore, and Learn ✳

Believe Manifesto

Create an affirmation, poem, or manifesto about believing in yourself. We've got an example for you that you're going to love! Check out this fabulous passage by Sarah Harvey: *A Badass, Truth-Soaked Manifesto to Help Us Live Like We Really Mean It.* This is an abbreviated excerpt:

> ***"I hereby undeclare the war on my own heart.***
>
> *I am done picking fights with my heart, raging epic battles with my soul and telling my intuition to shut the hell up.*
>
> *I am done denying who I really am.*
>
> *I'm done muting my roarin' goddess voice down to a hoarse, pathetic whisper. I'm done erasing my vibrant, neon colors and appearing to the world in scrambled frames of black and white. I'm done pretending I have no power, that I'm a helpless victim of circumstance, that I don't know how to rise like the bravest phoenix.*
>
> *That crap ain't gonna fly anymore.*

'Cause I can move mountains and I know it. Why deny it anymore?

It's time to live in juicy technicolor, with moonbeams woven in my hair, truth dripping from my mouth like mango juice and love oozing from my heart like a river of rubies that follows me everywhere—a raw silk scarf, a constant companion.

Gone are the days where it feels okay to recklessly abandon myself. Finished are the moments where it seems brilliant to destroy myself. Done are the years where I pleased everyone but myself.

I hereby undeclare the war on my own heart."

You've got goosebumps, right? Have fun coming up with your own passage to live by, or check out Sarah's full version on the web and print it out for inspiration!

Discovering Your Authentic Self

Authenticity takes self-exploration, understanding, and a willingness to slow down and learn about ourselves. Let's start by asking ourselves some questions.

- What do you love to do?
- How would you describe yourself?
- What are your values, goals, and strengths?
- What piques your curiosity?
- What gets you excited and motivated?
- What drains you and stresses you out?
- Do you get recharged when you're alone or around other people?

- Do you enjoy being outdoors or feel more comfortable indoors?

- What are the dreams you want to pursue?

- Where are the places you want to go?

Other avenues to learn about yourself are emotional IQ and personality tests. There are many free options available on the internet. Take a few different ones to help you see where your emotional strengths are and how to keep reinforcing and building upon those strengths. Be sure to journal about what you learn about yourself!

✳ Inspirational Quotes that Support This Mantra ✳

- "Working hard is important, but there's something that matters even more: believing in yourself."
    —Harry Potter

- "It is never too late to be what you might have been."
    —George Eliot

- "It is confidence in our bodies, minds, and spirits that allows us to keep looking for new adventures."
    —Oprah Winfrey

- "Praise and blame are all the same."
    —Richard Carlson

✳ Alternate Mantras for This Topic ✳

- Gotta be me.

- I am enough.

- I am constantly evolving.

- I undeclare war on myself.

✳ Songs to Add to Your Believe Playlist ✳

- "Be Yourself"
  by Audioslave

- "Beautiful"
  by Christina Aguilera

- "Born This Way"
  by Lady Gaga

- "Hercules"
  by Sara Bareilles

- "The Middle"
  by Jimmy Eat World

✳ Further Resources ✳

- *Be Yourself, Everyone Else is Already Taken*
  by Mike Robbins

- *The Courage to Be Yourself*
  by Sue Patton Theole

- *Self-Confidence Workbook: A Guide to Overcoming Self-Doubt and Improving Self-Esteem*
  by Barbara Markway and Celia Ampel

- *Unf*ck Yourself: Get Out of Your Head and Into Your Life*
  by Gary John Bishop

Humor is Healing

"Always laugh when you can; it's cheap medicine."
—Lord George Gordon Byron

Humor truly is healing medicine. This is no joke. There's scientific proof that laughing your ass off is really good for you. Of course, we know laughter feels good, but it's a plus when something that feels great is also good for us. The immediate and extended benefits of laughter are plentiful. It stimulates major organs, increases oxygen intake, releases feel-good endorphins, soothes tension, promotes muscle relaxation, and helps reduce physical symptoms of stress. In the long term, laughter improves your overall mood and immune system, relieves pain, and improves relationships. And the pièce de résistance: it improves feelings of self-worth and overall happiness! It does this by reducing cortisol, the stress hormone that causes a host of mental health and physical issues. When you embrace the lighter side of life, it provides insight, perspective, and, ultimately, a more positive outlook.

The medical community is taking notice of therapeutic humor and its healing benefits. One of our favorite health movements is called the *International Society for Humor Studies*. The therapists in this field coach people on how to laugh genuinely and fully as a coping strategy for dealing with life's stresses, such as unruly children, illness, money, or whatever else life throws at you. The idea is to teach people to use laughter to deal with things that usually do not make us laugh. Another health movement catching on in mainstream America is called *laughter yoga*. Dr. Madan Kataria, a charismatic physician from India, founded this form of yoga in 1995, and it's blossomed into more than six thousand laughter clubs in sixty countries around the world. The concept here is that even if you don't feel like laughing, go ahead and do it, and your body will be tricked into thinking something hilarious and happy is going on. It's true; laughing for no reason elicits the same psychological and physiological benefits as genuine laughter. Laughing is like a cardiac and stress relief workout for your mind and body. A good laugh gets the blood circulating and the lungs moving, which stimulates deep breathing. Plus, it's very difficult to hold onto anxiety and anger while you are doing it. So, next time you feel stressed out, go ahead and laugh it up. You'll feel better! Your brain and body will release happy chemicals, setting off your relaxation response. It's a fantastic and fun bottom-up approach that trains the mind through the body.

> **Remember and repeat:**
> ***Humor is healing.***

✳ Helene ✳

WE ALL HAVE people in our lives who lift our spirits with humor. Even if we've had a bad week or are feeling down, we find ourselves smiling in their presence. My dad is one of those people for me. Like many things, when I was younger, I didn't appreciate the awesomeness of this amazing quality. Now, when I spend the day with him, I come home with a twinkle in my eye, a lighter heart, and a smile deep down inside of me. Armed with the tool of laughter, I am ready to handle what life brings. When my son is around his grandpa, he laughs in delight and says, "Silly Grandpa," as he jokes with him. As I watch them together, I realize that my dad is passing on his gift to his grandson, that natural and effortless flair for humor that some have and thankfully share with others. Laughter plays such a huge part in my happiness that *Humor is healing* is one of my main go-to mantras inspired by one of the very best people I know (thanks, Dad. You will always be my laughter hero).

∼

Even in times of great despair, laughter magically continues to be medicinal. Life brings dark and disheartening events all too often. The American psychologist Gordon W. Allport says, "So many tangles in life are ultimately hopeless that we have no appropriate sword other than laughter." When it really comes down to it, why not give it a try? It certainly can't make it worse. When we are suffering, we need a break from our complex emotions. Laughter provides us with that break. Ironically, laughter distances us from our feelings but draws us closer to others. Do you have a friend or family member in your life whose sense of humor just cracks you up? Someone who infects you with their laughter? Then you know what we're talking about when we say the shared experience of laughter brings us closer to others.

Laughing with your partner strengthens the relationship, infusing good feelings and lovely chemicals such as endorphins and oxytocin (a.k.a. the cuddle hormone). It makes sense, right? If you are laughing with the person you love, feeling all good inside, it decreases any room for holding onto anger or resentment. So, when a loved one is angry at you, evaluate the situation and make amends, but it also doesn't hurt to make them laugh. Bring humor into the difficult moments. Shifting perspective from a negative situation to a humorous one diffuses negative feelings *fast*! Of course, with that said, the laughter has to be nonconfrontational, and the other person must find it funny! So, be humble when employing laughter-infused "let's make amends" behavior. Man, does it work. It is as good for them as it is for you. It brings on strong emotions, which provides the human connection we all thrive upon.

Now, for those of you out there reading this and thinking, *I don't have a sense of humor,* or *I am not funny, so this won't work for me,* we're here to tell you that you're not gonna get out of it that easily! A sense of humor, like any skill, can be strengthened or learned. Even if you grew up in a home that did not support humor or anything light and fun, that does not mean you can't reignite your inner child. The more you work out and flex your humor muscles, the stronger they will get. There are exercises inspired by laughter yoga and other fun elements at the end of the chapter that will help do just that! They are wonderfully holistic exercises that engage the abdominal muscles, lungs, and most other body systems. The key is your buy-in and willingness to let go of self-consciousness for a few moments. Hopefully, this mantra will motivate you to cultivate laughter whenever possible. It is so good for your health. So, go ahead and yuck it up. We give you permission to be silly and open your heart and mind to fun and laughter. Laugh until you cry or pee your pants. We promise you'll be glad that you did!

※ **It's Your Turn to Play, Explore, and Learn** ※

Old Man Hearty Laugh and Yawn

This exercise should have you and anyone you coerce into doing it feeling good in no time. You can even do it with your pet. First, take a moment to center your thoughts and let go of any apprehensions. Now, lean your head back, stretch your arms wide, and commence your best old-man over-the-top yawn. Think Monty Python over-the-top! The more ridiculous, the better! Really stretch your arms out, raise your chest up, and make it as obnoxious as possible. It's important to feel the pull and tightening all the way down into your pelvic floor.

Now, take a five- to ten-second break and repeat, but this time, add a jolly laughter to the end of the yawn. Like you are cracking up at your obscene yawning performance. This exercise triggers your vagus nerve, which stimulates your parasympathetic nervous system. You will feel tingles if you are able to stimulate it. Let the relaxation begin!

The Hawaiian (I Need a Vacation) Aloha Laughter

First, start by inhaling deeply. Then, stretch your arms and chest up toward the sky and say, *"Alo-o-o-o-o-o-o-o-o-o-o"* as you slowly exhale. At the very end of the exhale, say with gusto, *"Ha-a-a-a-a-a-a-!"* Add a little Hawaiian touristy hula dance to make it even more fun. Making your exhale longer than your inhale triggers that relaxation response and gives you the healing benefits of laughter. If you want to add some real action, during the *haaaaaa* sequence, fall into your bed face-first onto a soft pillow. Do this close to the bed, and make sure you'll land on your pillow. Safety first, peeps!

✻ Inspirational Quotes That Support This Mantra ✻

- "There is little success where there is little laughter."
  —Andrew Carnegie

- "We don't laugh because we're happy. We're happy because we laugh."
  —William James

- "In the end, everything is a gag."
  —Charlie Chaplin

- "If we couldn't laugh, we would all go insane."
  —Jimmy Buffet

- "Laugh it up, fuzzball."
  —Han Solo in *Star Wars, The Empire Strikes Back*

✻ Alternate Mantras for This Topic ✻

- Always laugh when you can.

- Laugh your ass off.

- Laughter is the best medicine.

- Life is better when you are laughing.

- We are here for a good time, not a long time.

✻ Songs to Add to Your Laughter Playlist ✻

- "Between a Laugh and a Tear"
    by John Mellencamp and Rickie Lee Jones

- "Sic 'em on a Chicken"
    by the Zac Brown Band

- "Friends in Low Places"
    by Garth Brooks
        (it makes us laugh and is a blast to sing along to!)

- "It Takes a Lot to Laugh, It Takes a Train to Cry"
    by Bob Dylan

- "Drunk on a Plane"
    by Dierks Bently

✻ Further Resources ✻

- *Animal Joy: A Book of Laughter and Resuscitation*
    by Nuar Alsadir

- *The Healing Power of Humor*
    by Allen Klein

- *Life Is Short—Wear Your Party Pants*
    by Loretta LaRoche

- Association for Applied and Therapeutic Humor: www.aath.org (check out their reading list)

- Dr. Kataria's Laughter Yoga: www.laughteryoga.org

- https://www.yogajournal.com/lifestyle/laughter-cure/

If you have a favorite comedian who tickles your funny bone, chances are they have written a book. We recommend that book(s) for you!

"Curiosity is the most powerful thing you own."
—Anonymous

LIFE CAN BE wonderful, fruitful, and rewarding. It can also be difficult, frustrating, and downright soul-sucking. Thank you, Captain Obvious, right? When you find yourself in a negative spiral, we recommend an incredibly simple yet impactful strategy: *engage your innate sense of curiosity*. Curiosity engages our brains in a whole new way. It helps us separate from our irrational, emotional thinking and pulls in sorely needed logic. Curiosity helps us to avoid reacting and getting angry about something that's not going our way. Give it a shot; instead of just going through the motions or getting frustrated by life's events, become an analytical scientist or detective and ask lots of questions. Why does . . .? How can it get better? How can it be different? What can I control? What is out of my control? What past experiences are influencing my reactions to this situation? If you're feeling run-down, act like a doctor who is on the case. What have I been eating? Have I been sleeping? Have I been exercising? Am I stressed out or working long hours? Am I worrying about something or someone? Being curious about why you feel the way you do is the first step in making changes that lead to feeling better. There are so many advantages to curiosity, from more positive moods and relationships to increased productivity and engagement with life.

As adults, we have a lot of responsibilities and expectations that don't exactly nurture wide-eyed curiosity. Consequently, it might be buried deep down inside of us. Kip Thorne, an American theoretical physicist and super smarty pants, wrote, "We're born with a curiosity about the universe. Those people who don't have a curiosity don't have it because it's gotten beaten out of them in some way." You said it, Kip! Adulting and life can be absurdly hard, and sometimes, it beats curiosity right out of our daily dealings. It doesn't help that regiment, routines, and schedules are what drive most industries today. Plus, our education system seems to value standardized test scores and GPAs as opposed to questioning, creativity, and exploration. This doesn't bode well for those with unique perspectives and ideas, otherwise known as innovators and inventors.

Curiosity killed the cat, but for awhile I was a suspect.
-Steven Wright

You've probably heard the saying, "Curiosity killed the cat." This old Irish proverb was used to deter people from investigating, questioning, or trying new things. This dire warning implied that if you were curious, bad things would happen to you. Basically, it dissuades us from being curious and tells us to mind our own business. We bet many of you have memories of parents or adults scolding your childhood self after you were caught in mischief. We would like to go on record that curiosity did *not* kill the cat. It's far more likely that curiosity is what made the cat playful, spunky, and living their best life!

Trauma is another curiosity killer because it puts us into survival mode. Most adults have gathered some traumas along life's path. But too much survival mode is not good for us. Take a moment and ask yourself, *When was the last time I was genuinely curious and invested in the pure wonderment of the inner workings of things?* If it's been a while, never fear. Remember neuroplasticity? That means we can forge new neural pathways and retrain our brains to be curious. It'll involve some self-awareness this time around, but curiosity is not dead; it is an ember waiting to be stoked and fired up again.

This mantra was inspired by our work as teachers and school counselors. We challenge students to become lifelong learners, doing our best to invoke curiosity as a form of self-investment. Curiosity is also an effective strategy to employ when we are learning about subjects that are out of our wheelhouse, or we have zero interest in learning about . . . geometry, anyone? Picture a literary student who wants to create stories and invent rich, complex characters but is required to take physics, chemistry, and statistics. Those aren't subjects they are innately drawn to, but good students will challenge themselves by approaching the material through the lens of curiosity and asking "why and how" questions. This type of invested learning piques the brain into actively engaging with the material. When students take the time to participate in this way, their investment will ultimately lead to better understanding. Curiosity can be more than just about academics or school. It can be about the hows and whys of your world. Go ahead and view your challenges through the lens of a curious observer!

> **Close your eyes and repeat,**
> *I will look at life through the lens of curiosity today.*

Being curious is also a type of grounding technique. Grounding techniques are strategies that get you out of your head and ground you in the present moment. You will get a nice little break from anxiety-inducing thought streams when you are observant of things going on around you. So, when you're feeling overwhelmed, we encourage you to step outside yourself and shift into a curiosity mode. It will allow you to hit the pause button and think clearly instead of reacting. Curiosity helps us to reframe how we see a moment, the day, a person, or even the world. It also stops our brain from conjuring up bullshit scenarios. Remember, when there is missing information, our brain will fill in the gaps and draw its own conclusions that are often flawed and unhelpful. So, before our minds start spinning wild tales, like the coach hates our kid or we definitely have elbow cancer, take a step back and think like a third-party observer. This step back allows space to shift our perspective, which is like finding a golden ticket!

Curiosity is also associated with higher relationship satisfaction because it increases our empathy and understanding. When one person shows genuine curiosity about another, that person, in return, views the curious person as more attractive. This makes sense because your desire to reciprocate naturally follows if someone actively listens and shows genuine interest in you. Additionally, curious people seek new adventures that challenge their worldview and fixed thinking patterns. The brain loves novelty and learning new things!

To sum things up, curiosity is an overlooked and underappreciated classic philosophy for dealing with difficulties. Admittedly, we are not pioneers in discovering this brand-new frontier. Plenty of people are in on this little secret. Bryant H. McGill, a social media influencer and author, said it best. "Curiosity is one of the great secrets of happiness." He's right! In a 2010 study, some very official and swanky researchers found that curious people are generally happier. It's not surprising because curiosity has been found to be associated with positive emotions time and time again. Curious? Do a little research, and work your curiosity muscles out!

✳ It's Your Turn to Play, Explore, and Learn ✳

The Case of the Curious Observer

Imagine a situation when you feel frustrated, angry, or defeated. Now, imagine the scene unfolding on a movie screen. As this tense scene plays, imagine yourself reaching for a remote control. This remote has a huge round knob located right in the middle, labeled *emotional level*. You are going to visualize yourself turning that knob all the way down. Imagine your feelings being dialed down to absolutely nothing. Now move to the second knob labeled *curiosity*. You are going to turn that bad boy all the way up. Time to put that heightened curiosity to work and start interjecting questions. Let's analyze this with elementary deduction and reasoning.

- What is the situation really about?

- What do I have control over in this scenario?

- What changes or adjustments can I make? Can I do something differently?

- What advice would I give the person on the screen to help them?

- Do I notice assumptions, storytelling, catastrophizing, or irrational emotional thinking?

- Why do I want _____ to change?

- Why am I doing what I do now?

- Why is it important to me?

Flex Your Curiosity Muscles

Check out these curiosity exercises and pick one that speaks to you!

- Bust out your journal and write down one country you have always wanted to visit. Now don the hat of an investigator! Learn about the country's cultural norms, must-see sites, and tourist destinations. What is the local cuisine? Where is the best place to sample these culinary delights? Investigate the currency, exchange rates, the best places to stay, and the best time to visit. Let your research take you in new directions. You'll see how fun curiosity can be!

- Write down a list of topics that interest you and set a goal to learn about or get involved in one or two of them. There is no wrong answer. Topics could include hiking trails, woodworking, yoga, musical instruments, side hustles, concerts, plants, alien sightings, healthy habits, dog breeds, Sepak Takraw (volleyball with no hands), worm charming (oh, it's fucking real friends), marine life, crime stats in Tasmania, etc. This will give your curiosity muscles a workout! After learning about or participating in a new endeavor, take time to write down and reflect on the benefits. If there is a barrier to getting started, break it down into smaller steps so you can still get a taste of what you are curious about. For example, start with an online yoga video instead of joining a class.

- Podcasts are *great* sources for stoking your curiosity. Experts, charismatic personalities, researchers, and scientists all share their greatest secrets, discoveries, and hacks! Podcasts are on all smart devices and use several platforms. Make a list of keywords to enter in the search bar. Here are a few examples to get you going: mental health, self-care, well-being, anxiety, holistic health, positivity, humor, mindfulness, meditation, positive thinking, psychological flexibility, gratitude, mind-body connection, perfectionism, and positive thinking. You may have to sift through a few to find a series that resonates with you, but it's worth it. Download or save a few of your favorites, the ones that engaged you and piqued your interest. You're much more likely to listen to something you have lined up and ready to hit play! Look for episodes that pique your curiosity, inspire you, or make you laugh. Listen to podcasts during your commute to work, while exercising, doing chores, or walking the dogs.

✶ Inspirational Quotes That Support This Mantra ✶

- "Curiosity and questions will get you further than confidence and answers."
  —Maxime Lagacé

- "Curiosity is the superpower for the second half of our lives—it keeps us learning, it keeps us asking questions, and it increases our self-awareness."
  —Brené Brown

- "Curiosity about life in all of its aspects, I think, is still the secret of great creative people."
  —Leo Burnett

- "Remember to look up at the stars and not down at your feet. Try to make sense of what you see and wonder about what makes the universe exist. Be curious. And however difficult life may seem, there is always something you can do and succeed at. It matters that you don't just give up."
  —Stephen Hawkings

✶ Alternate Mantras For This Topic ✶

- Curiosity leads to possibilities.

- Try being curious.

- Curiosity killed the cat? Nah, the cat died happy with all the answers.

- Look at life through the lens of curiosity.

✷ Songs to Add to Your Curiosity Playlist ✷

- "Car Radio"
    by twenty one pilots

- "Dog Days Are Over"
    by Florence & The Machine

- "Lasan"
    by Michael Kiwanuka

- "Mr. Curiosity"
    by Jason Mraz

- "Upside Down"
    by Jack Johnson

✷ Further Resources ✷

- *A Curious Mind: The Secret to a Bigger Life*
    by Brian Grazer and Charles Fishman

- *Curious?: Discover The Missing Ingredient to a Fulfilling Life*
    by Todd Kashdan

- *The Kind Self-Healing Book: Raise Yourself Up with Curiosity and Compassion*
    by Amy Eden Jollymore

- *Why?: What Makes Us Curious*
    by Mario Livo

- *The Benefits of a Curious Mind: The Role of Curiosity In Personal And Professional Development*
    by David Gilbert

"These things will be hard to do, but you can do hard things."
—Glennon Doyle

THERE ARE DAYS when we feel strong, competent, able to fight, hustle, and be feisty as all get out. But there are also days when we feel heavy, like an imposter, incompetent, and unprepared to deal with conflict, stress, and chaos. These days, it feels hard to get out of bed and just go through the motions. This mantra reminds us there is a brave warrior and a deep well of strength that resides in all of us. It helps shift us into a motivational mindset and reminds us that we have courage and determination. You have done hard things, and you can *still* do hard things, even things that feel fucking impossible. The payoff is not on the easy road; it's in overcoming our challenges.

The good, the bad, and the ugly are all a part of this one-shot deal of being human. Stress will happen, you will be challenged, and of course, you will get your ass handed to you from time to time. But there are good reasons for experiencing hardships. Doing hard things is actually good for us! It's healthy for our brain and body to be pushed, uncomfortable, and even tolerate pain. We're talking about things like workouts, research papers, cleaning the garage, cold plunges, or tackling a home renovation. Yep, too much of the good life is not always good for us. Hundreds of years ago, suffering was considered a part of life. In the last few decades, we have been pleasure seekers, avoiding discomfort at all costs. Now the pendulum is swinging back the other way, hopefully toward the middle, that hits the sweet spot of balance.

The message is that *moderation is key,* and excess in any form is not good. Many of us grew up with cultural messages telling us that having tons of money and taking it easy is the ticket to a good life. However, this message was continually challenged as we watched some of our favorite rich and famous personalities suffer from drug addictions, poor mental health, scandals, bankruptcies, divorce, and incarceration. The shine of being rich and famous began to tarnish, and people wondered if having everything was such a good thing. Still, the excess was, and still is, very much promoted. Think *Wolf of Wall Street*, *Vogue*, over-the-top parties, McDonald's supersizes, and Costco-size Peanut M&Ms. The cultural message is that *more makes you happier!*

As previously discussed, technological advances have allowed the medical community to more easily evaluate what prompts our mental health to thrive. Neuroscientists pulled back the curtain to reveal that our brains need a balance of ups and downs in life. We just are not meant to live in a state of effortless, blissful indulgence. Our brain does not like it one fucking bit. The brain goes haywire if the scale is tipped too far toward adversity (such as pain, exhaustion, stress, or workaholic behavior). If the needle is too far toward pleasure (such as doom scrolling, video games, eating whatever tastes good, spending money without saving, and laying on the couch watching movies all day), the brain does not function at its best. In today's "I want it now" culture, product is often stressed over process. We want to be healed after one therapy session. We want better abs in eight minutes. We want to master and excel at new activities right away. Unfortunately, it rarely works out that way. We're sure you've heard the saying that anything worthwhile takes time, right? This holds true for many things! We advocate for a life of balance, mixing in challenging tasks alongside the hedonistic indulgences we all love. The goal is to cultivate a stable, everyday life full of ups and downs. Anna Lembke, MD, promotes moderation in her remarkable book *Dopamine Nation: Finding Balance in the Age of Indulgence*. Her research confirms that the relentless pursuit of pleasure and avoidance of pain actually leads to difficulties and dissatisfaction. A good dose of abstinence restores the brain's reward pathway and our capacity to find joy in simple pleasures.

> **Inhale deeply and repeat,**
> *Doing hard things is good for me!*

✷ Beth ✷

ONE COLD JANUARY morning, in the middle of nowhere Northern New Mexico, I was riding in the passenger seat of a small truck. My family was riding quietly in the back seat, cruising over seventy-five mph, gazing out the windshield at the stars of a clear, moonless sky. The serenity of that early predawn morning was disrupted when an elk, sprinting down the side of a hill, ran out in front of the truck. The driver swerved, and then chaos erupted. The next few moments were a blur of bright lights, violent sounds, and the unforgettable smell of gas and smoke from the airbags. The truck had skidded off the road and plunged eight feet into a cement culvert, crumpling the truck's front end into nothingness. My memory is a mash of the sounds, smells, and eerie silence. It was like a war scene in a movie where a soldier is shell-shocked, wandering around dazed with muted sounds in the background.

I remember hearing strange voices talking to me. They were telling me to stay awake. I could hear a mix of my children's scared voices asking me if I was okay and the sound of people walking on broken glass. I was eventually cut out by the jaws of life and air-evacuated by helicopter to a hospital in Colorado. I'm still discovering different injuries from that day. A damaged right hip, torn labrums, torn tendons, and other shit you would think doctors would catch, but apparently, the bastards were mostly worried about keeping me alive. The nerve of some people, am I right?

Some days are ridiculously hard for me, and I would love nothing more than to stay in bed all day with a heating pad and muscle relaxers. However, I have learned that giving in to the easy is ultimately unhelpful if I want to engage in my life fully. Before this accident, I couldn't conceive of living through all of this and being happy. The me before the accident would have thought, *Nope, I can't do that,* and yet, now I know I can do *way* more than I think I can. I never understood when people would say a life-changing accident was an unexpected gift. I wouldn't go that far; if I had a magic wand and could wave away the accident, I would do it without hesitation. But since I am sans a magic wand, I deal with things the way they are.

I never remember feeling sorry for myself, and I still don't. I refused to be a victim because that is an easy mentality to fall into but crazy hard to climb out of! We all have a choice to face our challenges or turn away and blame others. The empowering option is obviously the first option. Face that shit head-on! Life is full of unexpected events that we can't even conceive of living through, but we do. We all have a well of inner strength waiting for us to tap into. Positivity and belief go a long way too. "Bounce Back" by Big Sean was my mantra and anthem! It was a bonus that my kids liked the song too, but we played that song all the time and sang the chorus as loud as we could, "Last night took an L, but tonight I bounce back."

Anthem and positivity aside, some days are still fucking hard, but I choose to fight and stay positive. I have learned that I can do hard things. This newfound confidence in my inner strength is one of those weird little gifts from the accident. I am less anxious and afraid, and I am more grounded. I now appreciate the power of gratitude, which brought my family closer together Still, it's not easy. Every morning when the damn alarm goes off at 5 a.m., I wake up and groan through the aches and pains, and then I get my ass moving. I know I can do hard things, and I will do my best to kick the day's ass with a bit of panache and a little sass! And if it's a bad day, I just say, "Last night I took an L, but tonight I bounce back."

So, take a moment to realize and acknowledge that you have the whole "you can do hard things" idea on reserve, ready to tap into it. While we don't have sharp fangs, cheetah speed, or a tough hide, *problem-solving* is our evolutionary superpower. This mantra is a rallying cry and reminder that you have everything you need to take on the hard stuff. You are capable. You are enough. You are a badass. It may not always look smooth and effortless, but you *will* move forward and learn from every failure. We encourage you to continue to fail forward. You have a deep well of strength, determination, and survival; it's all inside you, waiting to come to your aid. *It. Is. There.*

✴ It's Your Turn to Play, Explore, and Learn ✴

Strength Journaling

Strength journaling helps you push through your fears and realize *you will survive!* Gloria Gaynor figured this out in 1978 when the incredible "I Will Survive" disco song was first released. Ms. Gaynor is not the only one who can survive! This song is a battle cry for all of us, reminding us that we have survived and continue to thrive. The following strength journal prompts will help you solidify and magnify your belief that you can do hard things:

- Think of a recent tricky situation you had to navigate. Then, write it down in story format, and refer to yourself in the third person. Utilizing the third-person perspective is extremely helpful in giving you distance and stepping out of your story. Looking back over this challenging situation, how did this person cope? What strategies did they use to get through? What were the obstacles or challenges?

- Now, write a rave review of how that person handled the situation. Note what you admired about the person who survived the situation (yes, that would be you).

Hedonic Principle Override Challenge

Human beings are hardwired to move toward anything that our gut tells us feels good and shy away from things that might be uncomfortable. There's a region of the brain inside the basal ganglia that generates or inhibits neuron production in relation to pleasure and pain. That is not always a good thing! According to the hedonic principle, our emotional experience can act as a gauge that ranges from bad to good, and our brain's primary motivation is to *keep the needle on the gauge as close to good as possible*. Our brain's job is to keep us alive and avoid pain. However, it does not consider that some pain might be good for us; we're talking about things like facing our fears, being sore from building up our muscles, being uncomfortable in the face of something new, avoiding those high-calorie foods, pushing ourselves to go out of our comfort zone, etc. Sometimes, we have to override our natural preferences to stay safe so we can take on life's little challenges and kick ass by doing those hard things.

- Get a pen and paper and make a large "T," separating your paper into two columns. On the top of the paper, write down an activity you have been dreading and putting off. In column one, write down all the ways *not* doing this activity can cost you (loss of money, relationship, health, grades, etc.). In the other column, write down what would happen if you completed this task (feel good, be healthier, lose weight, have money, learn, etc.). Repeat this process for as many items as you'd like.

- Bust out your journal and look deeply into your motivations, reasons for procrastination, and the costs of inaction, and write down the feelings that come up for you. Are you afraid of physical or emotional pain? Are you worried about being hurt, uncomfortable, or out of your comfort zone?

- Come up with an action plan, and remember, sometimes you just have to rip the Band-Aid off quickly and *do* the hard thing. This process overrides the hedonic principle. In other words, you are overriding the brain's hard wiring for the greater good!

✳ Inspirational Quotes That Support This Mantra ✳

- "The road to success is always under construction."
  —Lily Tomlin

- "If you would only recognize that life is hard, things would be so much easier for you."
  —Louis D. Brandeis

- "Inaction breeds doubt and fear. Action breeds confidence and courage. If you want to conquer fear, do not sit home and think about it. Go out and get busy."
  —Dale Carnegie

- "You have to always continue to strive no matter how hard things get, no matter how troubled you feel. No matter how tough things get, no matter how many times you lose, you keep trying to win."
  —LL Cool J

✳ Alternate Mantras for This Topic ✳

- I am open to adversity.

- I am a resilient motherfucker.

- Hard is where growth happens.

- If it's easy, it ain't changing me.

- You can't have change without courage.

✳ Songs to Add to Your You Can Do Hard Things Playlist ✳

- "Don't Stop Believing"
  by Journey

- "Not Afraid"
  by Eminem

- "I Will Survive"
  by Gloria Gaynor

- "I'm Still Standing"
  by Elton John

- "Titanium"
  by David Guetta (featuring Sia)

✳ Further Resources ✳

- *Big Feelings: How to Be Okay When Things Are Not Okay*
  by Liz Fosslien and Mollie West Duffy

- *Do Hard Things: Why We Get Resilience Wrong and the Surprising Science of Real Toughness*
  by Steve Magness

- *Good for a Girl: A Woman Running in a Man's World*
  by Lauren Fleshman

- *How to Do Hard Things: Actual Real Life Advice on Friends, Love, Career, Wellbeing, Mindset, and More.*
    by Veronica Dearly
- *YOU Can Do Hard Things: How to Be Proactive With Your Growth and Not Reactive with Your Life*
    by Cynthia Caughie

"Some of us think holding on is strong;
but sometimes it is letting go."

—Hermann Hesse

Many of us are only comfortable when we feel in control. We want to control our feelings, events, and other people's feelings and choices. This desire for control inevitably leads us down the path of tension, stress, and unhappiness. The unknown makes life beautiful and interesting. Experiencing change means you are alive! So, the notion of being in control all the time goes against the very nature of life itself.

The following mantras are designed to help you interrupt yourself when the control bug gets ahold of you. Like so many things, letting go does not happen all at once. It happens a bit at a time and is a *conscious choice*. There is no magic wand, switch to flip, button to push, or pill to take. The process of letting go takes good old-fashioned work. We gotta practice awareness and consistently detour thoughts onto a more productive and positive road!

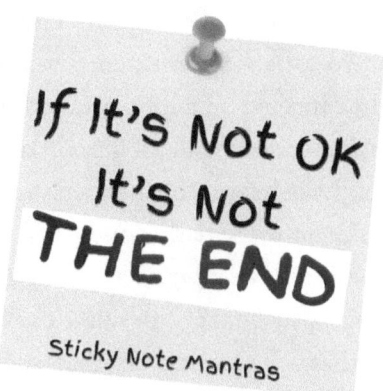

"Everything will be okay in the end.
If it's not okay, it's not the end."

—John Lennon

The daily stresses and drama of our lives can drain us and wear us down. While life doesn't always go as planned, we can choose to embrace outcomes or make ourselves miserable by ruminating over past events. If we could see five to ten years into the future, we would see that most of the time, everything works out all right. We all need to adopt a life philosophy that 99.9 percent of everything is going to eventually work itself out. Repeat to yourself, *It'll all work out in the end.* Weave it into your everyday thoughts, and you'll see a difference!

Self-doubt has this incredible knack of showing up when we least need it. Sometimes, it comes on suddenly; other times, it creeps up on us slowly like a late afternoon shadow. Some days, we feel invincible and that all things are possible. These are very good days. Then there are days we feel terrible, as though dark clouds hang over us. One of our songs that support this mantra is "Dancing Nancies" by The Dave Matthews Band. The following lyrics conjure up the image of clouds that sometimes dim our day "Dark clouds may hang on me sometimes, but I'll work it out . . ." Let's face it, we all have our dark cloud days. The key is to acknowledge your experience. Recognize and admit that it is simply one of those dark cloud days. Dark clouds can look like a trip to a packed emergency room, a flat tire on the way to work, a flight canceled on a long-awaited trip, a pipe breaking and flooding the inside of your wall, dog poop on the new rug, plans canceled, etc. As you have heard, shit happens, and it stinks! The key is to look up at the sky on those dark cloud days, see the blue peeking through, and *believe it will be okay in the end*. Time will move on, and eventually, things will change. Besides, dark clouds serve their purpose. We need them to remind us that sunny days are to be cherished and appreciated. The Chinese describe it as yin and yang. It's all about balance. We must have dark to have light, evil to have good, and ups to have downs. Dark clouds *will* happen, but having faith that the storm will eventually pass makes it easier to cope when there's a torrential downpour.

> **Breathe in deeply and repeat,**
> *It'll all be okay in the end.*

It's important to understand that we all hold the power to simplify our lives. Life itself is simple. It boils down to basic biological functions like air, food, sleep, and water. Those will sustain our bodies. Where it gets tricky and straight-up wackadoodle is when our brain gets involved. Our thoughts and perceptions are what give meaning to all the events in our lives. However, our minds love to skew the incoming data and dramatize stressful life events, usually making things feel worse. Using the phrase *It'll all be okay in the end* while going through a fender bender or some other unpleasant situation lessens the likelihood of building it up in our minds to a catastrophic event.

Often, when our mind blows things out of proportion, we are trying to control something that is out of our control. We want to be the engineer, architect, and builder to maintain control and design the outcome we desire. So, we try to control things that we simply can't control, and we do this exercise to make ourselves feel safe. That doesn't necessarily make it a healthy thing to do! Author Michael Singer wrote about his journey to find happiness. Mr. Singer let go and no longer focused his energy on the fruitless pursuit of trying to control everything. Instead, he directed his energy toward trusting in the process of living his own life. He writes, "How could I possibly explain the great freedom that comes from realizing to the depth of your being that life knows what it's doing?"

Ultimately, *we must fucking learn to let things go that are out of our control for our own sanity.* It really comes down to choice. Do we choose to stress, fret, worry, or freak out? Or do we choose to accept, do the best we can, and believe it will all work out? Life will move forward; some things can be influenced, and others cannot, but the day will move on to the next one regardless of our choice. It is our lifelong challenge and quest to figure out which one is which! When we do learn to let go and believe in the process of living a good life, our anxiety lessons, and the need to engineer outcomes fades away. Trust that whatever it is, it'll all work out in the end, and if it doesn't, well, then it's obviously not the end.

Take a moment to reflect on your experiences and times that caused you stress. For example, your house was not selling, your child didn't make the team, you lost your job, your significant other broke off the relationship, or your mom was angry with you. Those events probably seemed devastating, oppressive, or never-ending. Looking back on them, we know that things did work themselves out, one way or another, and life went on. It may not have worked out how you wanted, but you moved forward, and things are different now. We wouldn't say it worked out in cases of tragedy or loss, but no matter what happens in life, it does move on.

Accepting that time will move forward regardless of our outlook is empowering. It gives us the perspective needed to let go of anxiety and rumination. We can enjoy what life offers more easily when we are not stuck or fretting over things we cannot control. What could be more liberating than knowing that we don't have to be in control of everything? Why should we feel like Atlas with the world hoisted upon our shoulders when, in truth, we are not responsible for everything in our world? So many things in this world are impervious to our influence and demands. They change on their own accord, no matter how much we push, pull, hope, yell, or scream. A Chinese parable that has been passed down for thousands of years is one of our favorite illustrations of this idea. It's about a farmer who responds to life's events by saying, *"Good luck? Bad luck? Who knows?"* We actually have a friend who tattooed this phrase on her ass because she loved this idea so much.

> *"There is a Chinese story about an old farmer with an old horse for tilling his fields. One day, the horse escaped into the hills, and when all the farmer's neighbors sympathized with the old man over his bad luck, the farmer replied,* **'Good luck? Bad luck? Who knows?'**
>
> *A few nights later, the barn burned down. If the horse had been in the barn, it would have died.*
>
> *A week later, his horse returned with a herd of wild horses from the hills, and this time, the neighbors congratulated the farmer on his good luck. His reply was,* **'Good luck? Bad luck? Who knows?'** *Then, when the farmer's son was attempting to tame one of the wild horses, he fell off its back and broke his leg. Everyone thought this was very bad luck. Not the farmer, whose only reaction was,* **'Good luck? Bad luck? Who knows?'**
>
> *Some weeks later, the army marched into the village and conscripted every able-bodied youth they found there. When they saw the farmer's son with his broken leg, they let him stay home."*

So, if we accept that life is not black and white, embracing uncertainty and going with the flow is much easier. Accepting the things we cannot change or control is essential to a healthy outlook. Remember to acknowledge feelings of anger, disappointment, or hurt when things do not go your way, but eventually work around to saying, "Good luck? Bad luck? Who knows?" It's one of the alternate mantras for this topic, and if it resonates with you, then maybe you, too, will tattoo this phrase on your ass.

✳ Beth ✳

HAVING WORKED AS a high school counselor, I have witnessed a lot of students feeling utterly heartbroken when denied entrance into their dream college. Tears and grieving usually follow. I gently remind them that a specific outcome does not guarantee happiness. Many of these students return to campus for a visit a year or two later. More often than not, they will share with me how grateful they are to have landed at their current school, where they met their best friend, the love of their life, or landed in an amazing program. Had they gotten into their dream school, they would not have experienced these seminal moments. Whatever materializes, it is up to each individual to make the most of it. You can choose to believe that you are meant to be where you are, or you can resist changes and make yourself miserable. So, the next time you hope something will happen, or conversely will not happen—say to yourself, *I'll be okay either way.*

〜

This mantra also extends to the concept of worrying. Worrying is probably one of the most unproductive uses of energy. Absolutely nothing changes by worrying. It is the epitome of "spinning your wheels"—no outcome is achieved, nothing is gained, and an enormous amount of energy is expended for naught. Author Ernie

J. Zelinski explained in his book, *The Joy of Thinking Big*, "Worrying about things we can't control is wasted because we can't control them, and worrying about things we can control is wasted because we can control these things." Constant worrying can lead to a host of health-related challenges, such as depression, anxiety, stomach problems, and insomnia. However, current research says three-fourths of chronic worriers can change their habits using cognitive behavioral strategies, such as mantras! Go mantras!

In a way, this is a humbling mantra. Understanding that there are things in this universe that we cannot manipulate is frustrating but, at the same time, enlightening. This knowledge frees us to focus our energy on what we *can* control. True, things don't always work out the way we hope, but we do move on. Finally, we would be remiss if we didn't include this classic that has helped so many struggling with letting it go, the granddaddy of them all, The Serenity Prayer: *God, grant me the serenity to accept the things I cannot change, the courage to change the things I can, and wisdom to know the difference.*

☀ **It's Your Turn to Play, Explore, and Learn** ☀

Mindfulness Techniques to Let Go of Control

The renowned author and alternative medicine advocate Deepak Chopra encourages detachment from outcomes through mindfulness. When you think about it, a lot of anxiety comes from wanting a specific outcome, the one that's best for us or someone we care about, right? The shocker here is that what we feel is best for us is really just what we *want* to happen and what we *think* will bring us the most happiness. Let go of your attachment to the right or best path, and be mindful that there are all kinds of possibilities out there. Let these questions pique your curiosity and increase your awareness of this subject:

- What if you get precisely what you want, and then it turns out to be nonsense?

- What if you get something you would never imagine or dream of choosing, but it places you on a path to a richer life?

Make a conscious choice daily to spend less time worrying about specific outcomes. If you do, you will find that you are ready to accept change. Remind yourself that you are safe, and everything will be okay no matter how it works out. Then, when you break your leg and can't play hockey for the rest of the season or don't get the promotion you wanted . . . you might not be happy about it, but you'll adapt much more quickly and spend less time ruminating. A whole set of different opportunities open when you accept a different trajectory. We adapted a few more reflection questions from Tiny Buddha's *Letting Go of Control Worksheet*. These questions will help increase your mindfulness and identify areas in your life you are trying to control.

- Is there an emotional payoff in controlling a certain area of your life?

- How would your life improve if you let go of that control? What would you need to do differently?

- What would you need to believe about yourself, others, or the world to let go of that control in your life?

- What mantra inspires you when your dumbass brain returns to the same control pattern?

<u>Set Aside Worry Time</u>

This exercise redirects your worry to a particular time in your day. If you are having trouble sleeping because of anxiety, this will help you out. When worries pop up, tell yourself, *I'll save that for my worry time.* Habit stack by scheduling your worries for a certain time of day, such as when you wake up and have coffee. This allows you to cut down your worry time and focus on your actions or what you can control. Helen

Weng, a clinical psychologist and neuroscientist at the University of California San Francisco, mirrors this sentiment, suggesting that we're better off focusing on the intention of our actions rather than clinging to a particular outcome. "If you practice acting with intentions that align with your values (such as compassion, helping others, creativity), that may change what is happening, but you cannot expect a certain fixed outcome." Remember, the main goal is to always let go and focus on the process, not the outcome. We encourage you to write that down or highlight these words, *let go. Focus on the process, not the outcome.* Shoot, that would make a fantastic mantra, don't you think?

✻ Inspirational Quotes to Support This Mantra ✻

- "Eventually, all things fall into place. Until then, laugh at the confusion, live for the moments, and know everything happens for a reason."
    —Albert Schweitzer

- "Sometimes a 'mistake' can end up being the best decision you ever make."
    —Mandy Hale

- "You can't calm the storm, so stop trying. What you can do is calm yourself. The storm will pass."
    —Timber Hawkeye

- "Worrying does not take away tomorrow's trouble. It takes away today's peace."
    —Randy Armstrong

- "Everything will be alright does not mean everything will stay the same."
    —Unknown

✻ Alternate Mantra Ideas for This Topic ✻

- Good luck, bad luck, who knows?

- Hakuna matata.

- Be a warrior, not a worrier.

- Can I change it?

- Trust the process.

✷ Songs to Add to Your It's OK Playlist ✷

- "Dancing Nancies"
    by Dave Matthews

- "A Little Bit of This, A Little Bit of That"
    by Carolyn Dawn Johnson

- "That's the Way"
    by Jo Dee Messina

- "What I Can Not Change"
    by LeAnn Rimes

- "You Can't Always Get What You Want"
    by The Rolling Stones

✷ Further Resources ✷

- *Losing Control, Finding Serenity*
    by Daniel A. Miller

- *The Worry Cure: Seven Steps to Stop Worry from Stopping You*
    by Robert L. Leahy

- *The Joy of Thinking Big: Becoming a Genius in No Time Flat*
    by Ernie J. Zelinski

- *The END of WORRY: A Clinically Proven, 4-Step Protocol for Ending the Worry-habit, Forever*
    by Steve Bierman

"Don't make assumptions. Find the courage to ask questions and to express what you really want."

—Don Miguel Ruiz

We all do it. We all make assumptions; there's no ifs, ands, or buts about it. *Assume* is made up of the Latin words *ass*, *u*, and *me*; approximately translated, it means "to make an ass out of you and me." While assumptions don't *always* lead to making asses of ourselves, more times than not, they cloud our perspective and lead to negative, unproductive feelings that dampen our everyday experiences.

To understand the nature of assumptions, we must understand perceptions. Our perceptions are what create our realities. So, what one person perceives one way, another may see entirely differently. University students in the field of psychology have researched, experimented, and studied perceptions for many years. They've proven time and again that when people witness an accident, rarely do they report the event in the same way. Neither did they agree on the sequence of events they witnessed. They didn't even agree on who was at fault. What causes the discrepancies? In the field of communication, there's a term called *frame of reference*, which is a particular set of beliefs or ideas on which we base our decisions and judgments. *Our frame of reference is created by our experiences, beliefs, ethnicity, gender, and personalities.* So, in the example of the car accident, the witnesses' frame of reference influences how they remember the accident. Were they in an accident previously that was not their fault? Did someone they know suffer from an injury? Do they watch crime shows? Are they rich or poor? All of these things create a lens that distorts our perceptions. Winston Churchill stated, "Man will occasionally stumble over the truth, but usually manages to pick himself up, walk over or around it, and carry on." Man is ingenious at changing his vision of the world to comply with his perceived truth. So, we bend reality to fit our own schema. This is another of our many ingenious built-in defense mechanisms that protect our ego and ease our anxiety about an uncertain world.

Authors and researchers Ed Diener and Robert Biswas-Diener studied the lives of people living in poor neighborhoods in India. Western visitors were asked to estimate the quality of life where poverty, unemployment, inadequate health care, and hunger were daily realities. In every area given to rate, the Western visitors estimated that life in the slums was intolerable. However, this wasn't the case. The residents rated their lives as very average, even better than average. Does this sound surprising? Who would want to live in the slums? The researchers noted the critical error made by the visitors. They *assumed* all areas of life in these crowded, noisy, poor conditions would be hellish. However, the visitors disregarded the positive aspects of these people's lives—close family ties, large events, soccer games, and strong religious connections. The visitors' perceptions were clouded by assumptions of a Western standard of living.

> **Take a deep breath and repeat,**
> ***Assumptions are assholes!***

We make an array of assumptions daily, ranging from trivial to more involved. We attempt to interpret the motivations, thoughts, and actions of others, including those of our kids, spouses, friends, coworkers, and family. We also assume the meaning of events. It's human nature to examine a situation and circumstances, make judgments, and then determine how it will ultimately affect us. However, we must realize that our mind's conclusions are one of a million possible interpretations. Take a moment to consider some assumptions you make regularly that cause anger, confusion, or unhappiness. Here are examples to spark your brainstorming session:

- Sarah and her husband agreed that he would get up with the kids on weekends to give her a break. Despite this, Sarah assumes that her spouse thinks she should be getting up and handling the kids. She can't enjoy getting a few extra hours of rest because she assumes he has an unspoken expectation that she should take care of everything. From his perspective, he's glad he can do something to help her get a break for a change.

- Bob assumes his colleagues think he's not doing enough at work. Whenever one of them is around, he feels like he needs to prove himself. He finds himself rattling on about how much there is to do and all the hours he's put in at work. His colleagues are worried about their workload and haven't considered Bob's performance. They hate running into him because he doesn't stop talking about himself, and it's hard to break away from him.

- While at a red light, Naomi glances at the car next to her. She sees the driver make a grimacing, derogatory face in her general direction. Naomi assumes the driver is upset because she abruptly switched lanes a few streets back, and she believes that he made faces in response to her driving skills. *Thanks a lot, buddy,* she thinks. *I'm doing the best I can here. What a crappy morning. Why can't people be a little more understanding?* In reality, the guy was grimacing because his coffee mug leaked and spilled on his pants.

This classic parable paraphrased from Zig Ziglar's *See You at the Top* is another great example of how assumptions can lead to, in this case, harmless misunderstanding:

> *A little girl is watching her mom prepare a ham and notices she cuts the end off before putting it in the pan. "Mom, how come you cut the end off like that?" the little girl asks. "I don't really know, honey, that's the way my mom did it so I've always figured that's how you cook a ham," the mom replied. The curious little girl asked Grandma why she cut the end off the ham before putting it in the oven. Grandma smiled and said, "That's the way I saw my mother do it time and time again. Ask your great grandma." So, the little girl did. Great Grandma said, "I had to do that because I never had a roasting pan big enough for a whole ham."*

A general awareness that *we all make assumptions every fucking day* is instrumental in learning to extract oneself from the negativity they cause. As we said in the book's first section, awareness creates a needed pause to examine whether your brain is irrationally filling in the blanks. This pause can be scarce and challenging because, like our thoughts, assumptions happen automatically. Taking a moment to reflect by writing in your journal at the end of each day is a great strategy to create awareness. Consider that the assumptions your brain makes *all* have the potential to shift and become new insights. For example, *She is being rude because she doesn't like me.* Or *He intentionally undermined my authority when he started the meeting without me.* This is a great moment to pause, reflect, analyze, and repeat, *I cannot assume.*

> **Take another cleansing breath and repeat,**
> ***Assumptions are assholes!***

After becoming more familiar with practicing awareness, you can add in some fancy strategies. A terrific one that brightens your attitude and general outlook is called *attributing positive intent.* Since we make up our assumptions, why not assume the best? It certainly couldn't hurt. In Naomi's situation in the car, she could have assumed the guy was having a bad day instead of attacking her driving skills. We make it up, so why not flip the script? This is especially handy with young children since we can't ask them what they were thinking when they said or did something hurtful (we can, but we may get an unhelpful response).

The work of developmental psychologist Dr. Becky Bailey encourages parents and caregivers to give children the benefit of the doubt when they are displaying those lovely behaviors that push your buttons. You know what we're talking about —temper tantrums, biting, kicking, crying, or being out of control. After you've taken a time-out and calmed down, revisit the incident, set boundaries, and attribute positive intent. This doesn't excuse the behavior, but it puts a positive spin on an otherwise negative situation. For example, "You were upset. You didn't know what to do, so you hit Mommy. No hitting. If you're upset, you can _____" (fill in the blank with how you'd like your kid to behave). In this scenario, by saying "you didn't know what to do," as opposed to "you were being plain evil and planned the whole thing out on paper," you are attributing positive intent. Try it out, and it will make both of you feel better. Once you get good at this strategy, you will find it easier to use in all aspects of your life. This also goes for those assumptions you tell yourself. *Our mind makes it all up,* and most of the time, it's unhelpful and self-defeating. Remember, our brain naturally creates assumptions that exaggerate our worst fears and insecurities. In other words, they're a bunch of BS! Think about how different your life would be if you changed the stories you tell yourself. What if you started telling yourself it's okay to be happy with how your life is right now? What if you decided you didn't have to compare your life to everyone else's? Awareness is the bomb here. Once we're aware of our assumptions, we can change those bitches!

Communication is a key ally in combating assumptions. Yes, it's *easier* to blame others, but it's not helpful and usually harmful to relationships. Most people think boundary setting is harsh and will lead to other people not liking them. We're here to tell you that you *can* be accepting of others and show compassion while setting boundaries. Just be mindful not to attack who they are as a person, which is a knee-jerk reaction when you feel like you're being treated like shit. Separate who they are from what they are doing. So instead of "you're such an asshole," shift to "I feel like we're not connecting, and that's important to me. Can we take some time to sit down and talk?" So, if you want to connect with others, you must communicate what makes you feel valuable and heard. A big part of that connection is holding others accountable. Setting boundaries may seem hard at first, and guess what? It is! It requires thoughtful effort and a dash of bravery, but setting boundaries from the get-go makes it easier in the long run. You're doing the hard work by laying the ground rules. Once you have, everything about the situation will get much easier because you have established those boundaries! We promise!

✳ It's Your Turn to Play, Explore, and Learn ✳

People Watching

We are meaning-making machines. We have some mad skills in this area! Familiarity makes us assume certain things even when they're not there. Our minds superimpose their own visualization of how things are. So, for this exercise, we will be detectives of *what is*. Find a good people-watching spot at a coffee shop, lunch spot, or grocery store. Going for a walk is also a great opportunity for people-watching. Try to separate your judgmental mind from *what is fact* or *missing information*. Remember, your mind loves to fill in those blanks! Your preconceived notions influence the way you see just about everything, so it isn't easy. But by questioning and becoming aware of your assumptions, they won't cloud your viewpoint quite as much.

Challenge Your Assumptions

Our brains are hardwired to make judgments about ourselves, situations, events, and others based on our previous experiences. We come up with our own "truths." The difficulty is that they are often inaccurate and unhelpful. In your journal, brainstorm areas where you might be guilty of making assumptions. List all the assumptions you routinely make, and consider how they affect your well-being. Writing it down helps you notice patterns or themes. Here are some guidelines to help you as you challenge your assumptions:

- Be a curious observer. Take an objective perspective.

- *Pause* before you respond to others to consider your assumptions.

- Ask questions whenever possible.

- Decide to see positive intent.

- Accept that others have a different belief system and way of communicating than you.

※ **Inspirational Quotes That Support This Mantra** ※

- "Don't build roadblocks out of assumptions."
   —Lorii Myers

- "Communication must be HOT. That's Honest, Open, and Two-way."

—Dan Oswald

- "The harder you fight to hold on to specific assumptions, the more likely there's gold in letting go of them."
    —John Seely Brown

- "Begin challenging your own assumptions. Your assumptions are your windows on the world. Scrub them off every once in a while, or the light won't come in."
    —Alan Alda

✳ Alternate Mantra Ideas for This Topic ✳

- Lack of communication breeds assumptions.

- Let go of your assumptions.

- Assuming the best can't hurt.

- Challenge my assumptions.

- The opposite of investigation is assumption.

✳ Songs to Add to Your Assumption are Assholes Playlist ✳

- "Assumptions"
    by Sam Gellaitny

- "Before You Accuse Me"
    by Eric Clapton

- "Don't Laugh at Me"
    by Home Free and Mark Wills

- "Don't Believe Everything You Think"
    by Lee Brice

- "What It's Like"
    by Everlast

✽ Further Resources ✽

- *The Four Agreements: A Practical Guide to Personal Freedom*
    by Miguel Ruiz

- *Shattered Assumptions: Towards a New Psychology of Trauma*
    by Ronnie Janoff-Bulman

- *Trapped by Assumptions: How to Break Mental Traps and Keep Your Mind Sharp (The Anchor of Our Purest Thoughts)*
    by Dr. Chong Chen

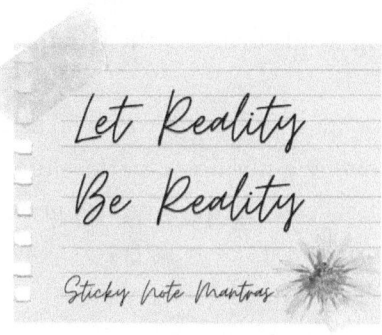

Let Reality Be Reality
Sticky Note Mantras

"Life is a series of natural and spontaneous changes.
Don't resist them—that only creates sorrow.
Let reality be reality.
Let things flow naturally forward in whatever way they like."
—Lao Tzu

ADAPTING TO CHANGE is something we have to muster up the courage and energy to do repeatedly. And it's hard. Like . . . really goddamn hard. The brain constantly creates pictures and narratives of how we believe things should be; when our expectations are unmet or change happens, we must adjust. If we don't learn to embrace this process, our mind gets a little wonky and launches into the nebulous realm of what could have been, should have been, would have been, or might have been. Steeped in rumination, the land of "if only" is a crappy, frustrating, and lonely place to be. Reflection is a double-edged sword, sometimes helpful and sometimes grossly unproductive. When you're stuck in a useless overthinking mode, use this mantra to cue your mind to stop resisting what is. Making a conscious choice to accept change decreases your stress levels and allows you to get more out of your present experiences.

Learning different ways to make peace with change is worthwhile since, let's face it, folks, change is not going anywhere! We like to think about change as finding ways to help ourselves say goodbye to the past. Patty Loveless's "How Can I Help You to Say Goodbye" is a wonderful illustration of this idea. She sings about difficult changes in a woman's life, and during tough times, she calls her mom. Her mother's comforting words make up the refrain:

> "I called up mama and she said time will ease your pain
> Life's about changing nothing ever stays the same
> And she said how can I help you to say goodbye?
> It's okay to hurt, and it's okay to cry
> Come let me hold you and I will try
> How can I help you to say goodbye?"

This song acknowledges and validates the pain that accompanies some changes. The source of emotional pain may be the loss of a loved one, a friendship, a job, health, the end of a relationship, financial loss, or unmet expectations. No matter what kind of change it is, we encourage you to seek out ways to help you move forward or *say goodbye* to the issue.

> **Breathe in and repeat,**
> *Let reality be reality.*

Self-care is paramount when going through a significant change or loss. Explore activities that soothe your soul, such as art, music, or being in nature or a place of worship. Finding a tangible reminder that symbolizes your loss, such as a talisman or piece of jewelry, can also be helpful. When you hold it, think of all your positive memories, or think of it as a token that encourages you to let go. Rituals can be a comforting and powerful way to let go of the past. For example, letting go of floating lanterns, creating a memory box, planting flowers or trees, or writing a letter. Staying connected with others is an integral part of self-care. If you isolate yourself, it may take longer to adapt to changes. Our nervous system is hardwired for connection. Our connections encourage neuroplasticity, which, as we've mentioned, stimulates new areas in the brain. When you connect, you get different perspectives and viewpoints. As you fold these into your outlook, your brain becomes more flexible. So, reach out to others when you are going through a hard time. Reaching out for help is not weak—that's just bullshit! Instead, think of asking for help as a sign of strength and confidence because it is! We are *all* better together!

Arthur Rubinstein said, "Of course, there is no formula for success, except perhaps an unconditional acceptance of life, and what it brings." Unconditionally accepting change sounds like a phenomenal plan. It is a worthy aspiration that we should strive for, but we should do so with the knowledge that it is a slow, gradual process. The pain of a loss or change can be staggering, and that pain may stay with us. As Patty Loveless implied in her song, time is a great healer. As we begin to find acceptance, the pain fades. As humans, we are damn resilient. We can use our connections with others, our mantras, and self-care strategies to help us move forward.

∗ Helene ∗

WHEN I WAS teaching special education, one of my student's mothers gave me this spot-on passage about the acceptance process called Welcome to Holland. It speaks of situations in life when reality doesn't quite match our thoughts and daydreams about how life is supposed to be. It's okay to mourn our expectations and be sad when shit doesn't go down as planned. When our picture-perfect life turns out less than perfect, we sometimes miss the truth—we're the ones who created those ideas and expectations. Our brain continues to generate these idyllic notions of a pain-free, worry-free life even after we have sternly told it to knock that shit off.

Welcome to Holland by Emily Perl Kingsley

©1987 by Emily Perl Kingsley. All rights reserved.
Reprinted by permission of the author.

I am often asked to describe the experience of raising a child with a disability—to try to help people who have not shared that unique experience to understand it, to imagine how it would feel. It's like this . . .

When you're going to have a baby, it's like planning a fabulous vacation trip—to Italy. You buy a bunch of guidebooks and make your wonderful plans. The Coliseum. The Michelangelo David. The gondolas in Venice. You may learn some handy phrases in Italian. It's all very exciting.

After months of eager anticipation, the day finally arrives. You pack your bags and off you go. Several hours later, the plane lands. The flight attendant comes in and says, "Welcome to Holland."

"Holland?!?" you say. "What do you mean Holland?? I signed up for Italy! I'm supposed to be in Italy. All my life I've dreamed of going to Italy."

But there's been a change in the flight plan. They've landed in Holland and there you must stay.

The important thing is that they haven't taken you to a horrible, disgusting, filthy place, full of pestilence, famine and disease. It's just a different place.

So, you must go out and buy new guidebooks. And you must learn a whole new language. And you will meet a whole new group of people you would never have met.

It's just a different place. It's slower-paced than Italy, less flashy than Italy. But after you've been there for a while and you catch your breath, you look around . . . and you begin to notice that Holland has windmills . . . and Holland has tulips. Holland even has Rembrandts.

But everyone you know is busy coming and going from Italy . . . and they're all bragging about what a wonderful time they had there. And for the rest of your life, you will say "Yes, that's where I was supposed to go. That's what I had planned."

And the pain of that will never, ever, ever, ever go away . . . because the loss of that dream is a very, very significant loss.

But . . . if you spend your life mourning the fact that you didn't get to Italy, you may never be free to enjoy the very special, the very lovely things . . . about Holland.

✳ Helene, cont. ✳

THIS STORY RESONATES with me in so many ways. Most significantly, it speaks to my journey with chronic pain that started in my late thirties. I think searching for an official diagnosis has been one of the most frustrating parts of my journey, leading to a smattering of tests, diagnostic procedures, shots, lifestyle changes, alternate therapies, medication, and a few surgeries to try and fix me. My husband and family have been absolute saints in going through all this with me. So, adapting to chronic pain has been one of my biggest challenges in life. I was very active and loved running, hiking, mountain biking, and kickboxing. But I use mantras, awareness, gratitude, connections with others, writing, and other tactics to deal with it. Yeah, I've built up my repertoire over the years. I'm working on treating pain like an old friend I recognize and say "hello" to instead of automatically jumping into survival mode and making it worse. This kind of acceptance goes a long way for me, and I can *let reality be reality* a little bit easier. The grief will always be there for the loss of my health, and that's okay.

> **Breathe in and repeat,**
> *Let reality be reality.*

Your brain takes time to adjust when going through the process of acceptance. Let's say you just lost someone you loved. There is an absence, and you feel like you've lost a part of yourself, right? That's because your brain codes your relationship with that other person as a "we." In other words, who you are is tied to who they were. When that person is gone, you must figure out how to operate with a new set of rules. The same goes for your identity when you lose a job, end a relationship, or have constant asshat pain. Emotions get magnified when you are grieving until your brain makes sense of what is going on. Grief doesn't go away. It stays with you, tied to memories and even future events. For example, *I wish my dad were here with me at my graduation. I wish I could be fighting that wildfire with my old crew*, or *I wish I could have sex as I did before that pelvic floor dysfunction.* However, our relationship with grief changes. The first 150 times you experience grief, when it knocks you on your ass, might be different than the 151st time when you think, *This blows, but I know what these feelings are.* Your brain is making connections that things are different little by little.

It can be comforting to know that things you lose stay a part of you. Literally, your brain's wiring changes. Your neural connections and proteins are permanently altered. You carry them in your brain, impacting your life, how you live, how you view the world, and what you value. Elisabeth Kubler-Ross, the psychiatrist who broke down grieving into the five stages of denial, anger, bargaining, depression, and acceptance, said, "The reality is that you will grieve forever. You will not 'get over' the loss of a loved one; you will learn to live with it. You will heal and you will rebuild yourself around the loss you have suffered. You will be whole again, but you will never be the same. Nor should you be the same, nor would you want to." The idea is that you will adapt, and it will become blended into who you are.

✳ It's Your Turn to Play, Explore, and Learn ✳

My Adaptation Plan

It's good to have a plan. Writing what you can do to ease your pain is helpful whether you're dealing with the loss of a loved one, health, friendship, a relationship, or an expectation. It gives you concrete ideas when you're overwhelmed and uncertain. So, brainstorm the following ideas to have on hand when sad, upset, or overwhelmed.

- Positive things I can say to myself . . .

- People I can talk to . . .

- My top coping strategies and self-care ideas . . .

✶ Inspirational Quotes That Support This Mantra ✶

- "Most things will be okay eventually, but not everything will be. Sometimes you'll put up a good fight and lose. Sometimes you'll hold on really hard and realize there is no choice but to let go. Acceptance is a small, quiet room."
  —Cheryl Strayed

- "The measure of intelligence is the ability to change."
  —Albert Einstein

- "In any given moment we have two options: to step forward into growth or step back into safety."
  —Abraham Maslow

- "The more you resist, the more you suffer. The more you accept, the more you grow."
  —Eckhart Tolle

✶ Alternate Mantras ✶

- What you resist persists.

- The song has ended, but the melody lives on.
- Go with the flow.
- Pain will pass.
- Adapt or die!

✻ Songs to Add to Your Acceptance Playlist ✻

- "Let It Be"
    by the Beatles

- "Tears in Heaven"
    by Eric Clapton and Will Jennings

- "How Can I Help You to Say Goodbye"
    by Patty Loveless

- "Life Changes"
    by Thomas Rhett

✻ Further Reading ✻

- *Grieving Brain: The Surprising Science of How We Learn from Love and Loss*
    by Mary-Frances O'Connor

- *Option B: Facing Adversity, Building Resilience, and Finding Joy*
    by Sheryl Sandberg & Andy Grant

- *It Was Always Meant to Happen That Way*
    by Brooke Castillo

- *Emotional Resilience: Simple Truths for Dealing with Unfinished Business of Your Past*
    by David Viscott, MD

> "Forgiveness lifts the weight of thoughts
> and feelings that no longer serve you.
> It makes room for hope, inner peace, and love."
>
> —Katrina Mayer

ANGER, PAIN, AND guilt are natural emotions. They are part of being human, so we all experience them. They are involved in the process of forgiveness. But, if we are stuck in these emotions for extended periods, it weighs us down. Staying in the weeds of heavy, negative emotions takes its toll on us emotionally and physically. Our moods become stagnant, and our bodies wear down. It ultimately leads to not-so-fun challenges like depression, anxiety, and immune system meltdowns. It isn't easy, but forgiving and letting go promotes growth, healing, peace, and balance.

Lewis B. Smedes, renowned Christian author, ethicist, and theologian, wrote, "To forgive is to set a prisoner free and discover that the prisoner was you." How true! Holding onto grudges and hate causes your brain to produce heightened levels of stress chemicals like our friends cortisol and norepinephrine. Besides making you feel terrible, the longer you harbor these feelings, the more difficult it is to think about your feelings. The good news is that there's a process to forgiveness, and once you do it, it's stored in your basal ganglia so you can do it again! It entails making a conscious decision to forgive. Deliberately acknowledge that we all deserve forgiveness because it's human nature to fuck up. Studies have shown that when individuals choose to forgive, it's strongly correlated with relief and peace. First, your brain will drop some dopamine into your system. Then, you'll have better blood circulation, less stress, better cognitive functions, and less chance of falling over with a heart attack. It does take time and energy to stop our thoughts from dwelling on the negative, wave the white flag, and head down the path of forgiveness. But moving toward a place of inner peace is priceless. Like all worthwhile things, moving forward requires a *conscious* effort of thought, will, and action.

Undoubtedly, some acts of forgiveness are more complicated than others. The father who forgives the man who murdered his son, the daughter who forgives her mother for putting her up for adoption, or the lover who forgives her unfaithful partner—these are as tough as they get. No one says it has to happen all at once. Simply work on making small, conscious steps on the path to forgiveness. You might have other emotions to manage, like grief and anger, before moving into acceptance and forgiveness. Taking time to acknowledge your feelings will help you move through them. Even if you feel anger concerning something less catastrophic, if it is hurtful to you, it triggers stress. For instance, you overhear a coworker criticizing you. It's not that big of a deal, but that shit hurts. Refocusing on the thought that we all deserve forgiveness is the key to taking heavy weights off our shoulders and moving forward on the path of personal growth.

It is almost a point of enlightenment when forgiveness becomes an option, knowing that by releasing hate and anger, you are releasing that person's hold over you. It is a common theme in religions to forgive the sins of those who have trespassed against us. You might even say it is ancient wisdom. Different cultures have written about forgiveness for thousands of years. It's unclear when the old "forgive and forget" cliché emerged, but it's misleading. Forgiving does *not* have to mean forgetting, especially when someone is attempting to forgive a more serious offense. And you're not excusing another person's actions or permitting them to do it again. Especially with survivors of abuse or trauma, the idea is to accept that what happened wasn't your fault. The memory is still a part of you and elicits strong emotions and visceral reactions. Try saying, "I will remember and recover, not forgive and forget." In recovery, your feelings get desensitized as you focus on new thoughts and perspectives, but they are still a part of you.

As we learn to forgive others, it encourages us to practice self-forgiveness. Too often, we hold shame and guilt about past transgressions, mistakes, and plain old bad choices. Forgiving yourself lightens your load and lets you move forward. Dr. John Delony, national best-selling author and mental health expert, describes unforgiveness as carrying a collection of bricks in a backpack that you must drag around everywhere you go. These can be little things or more serious offenses. Didn't handle something well with your kids? A brick is added. Got a DUI? There goes a heavy one. Feeling ashamed because you haven't exercised this week? Plop. Overeating or overindulging? Plop, plop. As you walk around, this collection of bricks will drag you into despair, affecting your ability to give and receive love. Start to take each brick out and scrutinize it, learn from it, and *lay it down* because being unwilling to forgive affects your relationship with yourself *and* others. Holding on to the false belief that you cannot forgive prevents you from

Toss those bricks!

living and being grounded in the present. It also causes bitterness, immobilization, and toxicity. We hope this mantra inspires you to lay down any bricks in your life or, better yet, chuck them from a tall mountain. Acknowledge that being human comes with making mistakes. Offer forgiveness to yourself and others. You'll be able to move on more easily, knowing that forgiveness is necessary because we are all perfectly imperfect. As Paul Boese eloquently said, "Forgiveness does not change the past, but it does enlarge the future."

> **Close your eyes and repeat,**
> *I will forgive myself and others.*

* Helene *

I HAVE HAD so many battles with forgiveness. One of my favorite (anonymous) quotes is, "I never make the same mistake twice. I make it like five or six times, you know, just to be sure." Yep—that's me. I've seriously fucked up and vehemently regretted the choices I've made, especially concerning my health. Those choices led to depressing consequences and put me in situations I never thought possible. Forgiving myself isn't easy because those consequences live on. I'd have to write another book to fill you in on all the sordid details. My go-to mantra song for this topic is "I'm Movin' On" by Rascal Flatts. I put it on time and again to help me to move forward. Please check out the whole song if you are dealing with forgiveness. Here are some of the first lines:

> *I've dealt with my ghosts, and I've faced all my demons*
> *Finally, content with a past I regret,*
> *I've found you find strength in your moments of weakness*
> *For once, I'm at peace with myself*
> *I've been burdened with blame,*
> *trapped in the past for too long*
> *I'm movin' on*

These words resonate deeply with me. They make me realize that keeping myself in the past doesn't help, and moving forward *makes room* for the future. J.K. Rowling said, "Rock bottom became the solid foundation on which I rebuilt my life." Rock bottom can be a rebirth from the ashes once you get past humiliation, guilt, and self-loathing. The only way to go is up. Accepting the consequences of my decisions, acknowledging my fallibility, and believing I am worthy of love and forgiveness, just like everyone else, helps me through the process.

~

Forgiving ourselves is one of the most terrifying and daunting challenges we can face. Taking an honest look inward at our less-than-stellar moments can be uncomfortable. But the payoff is incredible. Healing those deep wounds and releasing self-damning feelings of shame puts us on the path to inner peace. This release helps buffer us from negativity, and our newfound sense of contentment brings positivity to others. This positivity can potentially influence more individuals than you may have imagined due to the butterfly effect. There's a story about a therapist in a Hawaiian prison that exemplifies this idea beautifully. Dr. Hew Len, a student of the Hawaiian Ho'oponopono tradition, was on a personal journey to learn about self-compassion and self-forgiveness. However, the story gets really interesting when Dr. Len's journey not only transforms his inner world but also radiates out and influences the inmates he is working with. However, the story gets really interesting when Dr. Len's journey not only transforms his inner world, but it also radiated out and influences the inmates he was working with. Are you saying to yourself Hop-ah-Who? Because we did when we first heard about this! Ho'oponopono means *to make things right*. It is an ancient traditional Hawaiian practice of offering forgiveness that is still practiced today by many native Hawaiians. Ho'oponopono challenges everyone to turn inward and ask for self-forgiveness instead of looking outside themselves for the cause of their woes. Dr. Len offered forgiveness to himself, and consequently, he radiated peace, love, and kindness outward. His intentions of love and forgiveness encouraged the inmates to be open to self-forgiveness as well.

> **Breathe in and repeat this Ho'oponopono prayer to the universe,** *I'm sorry. Please forgive me. Thank you. I love you.*

The takeaway from Dr. Len's work is this: when you forgive yourself and cultivate inner peace, the outside world will reflect that peace. If you've been struggling with unhappiness, instead of blaming others, be curious about the practice of Ho'oponopono. Carve out some time for self-love and self-forgiveness exercises. When you strive to nurture your inner love, don't be surprised to find it reflected by those around you.

✻ It's Your Turn to Play, Explore, and Learn ✻

Write a Letter to Yourself

A great exercise to encourage self-forgiveness is to write a letter to the person you were in your past. Of course, you can also use this in relation to forgiving others by addressing the letter to the individual you are struggling to forgive. We've listed an example for you below.

Dear Me Ten Years Ago,

> *Hindsight is a beautiful gift! I now understand a lot about you that I never could have understood at the time. I now see that you weren't just flighty and irresponsible; you were having a rough time finding out who you were and your place in the world. I understand that some of the relationships you chose were not the healthiest or most stable for you, but I think those experiences made you the strong and wise person you are today. The hurt and pain proved the words, "What doesn't kill*

you makes you stronger." I can tell you that you will be much stronger in ten years. Don't even doubt that for a second!

This letter is to let you know that I forgive you for holding on to lost love, for crying at night when he left you, and for feeling sad for a very long time. I admire you because you picked yourself up and had the guts to start a new career. Eventually, you will find the love of your life! I promise! I want you to know I love the me of ten years ago. I'm sorry you had such a hard time, but I forgive and understand you, and I promise things will only improve. Be strong!

Me, Ten Years Later

<u>The Empty Chair Technique</u>

Fritz and Laura Perls, the founders of Gestalt Therapy, developed this exercise. It encourages individuals to become aware of their thoughts and reactions. If you're trying to forgive someone else, you're going to arrange two chairs facing each other. You sit in one chair and imagine the person you are upset with in the empty chair. Work on really seeing that person in the chair listening to you.

Now tell that person everything—why you're pissed off, how it's affecting your life, and any other feelings or messages you want to communicate. Then, switch chairs and become the offender. Put yourself in their shoes. Pretend to see things from their viewpoint, even if they're a dumbass, and make sure to have them issue you an apology. Go back and forth between the chairs until you get everything out. The same goes if you're trying to forgive yourself, but act as your inner critic first and then switch to your wise counselor.

✸ **Inspirational Quotes That Support This Mantra** ✸

- "Getting over a painful experience is much like crossing monkey bars. You have to let go at some point in order to move forward."
  —C.S. Lewis

- "There's no red, green, or blue pill for forgiveness. No quick fix. Forgiveness takes learning to lean on the source while taking life one day at a time."
    —Poet K.D. Gates

- "Watch out for each other. Love everyone and forgive everyone, including yourself. Forgive your anger. Forgive your guilt. Your shame. Your sadness. Embrace and open up your love, your joy, your truth, and most especially your heart."
    —Jim Henson

- "You only have to forgive once. To resent, you have to do it all day, every day."
    —ML Stedman

✷ Alternate Mantra Ideas for This Topic ✷

- Forgiving does not mean forgetting.

- Forgiveness lets me show compassion.

- Remember and recover.

- I am worthy of forgiveness, and so are others.

- Forgiving brings peace.

✷ Songs to Add to your Forgive Playlist ✷

- "I'm Moving' On"
    by Rascal Flatts

- "Forgive"
    by Rebecca Lynn Howard

- "Life's for the Living"
    by Passenger

- "Some People Change"

by Kenny Chesney

- "Wasted"
  by Carrie Underwood

✷ Further Reading ✷

- *Forgiveness: How to Make Peace With Your Past and Get on With Your Life*
  by Sidney B. Simon

- *Forgiving Troy: A True Story of Murder, Mental Illness and Recovery*
  by Thom Bierdz

- *The Railway Man: A True Story of War, Remembrance, and Fogiveness*
  by Eric Loma

- *Why Good Things Happen to Good People: How to Live a Longer, Happier, Healthier Life by the Simple Act of Giving*
  by Stephen Post, PhD, and Jill Neimack

MANTRAS TO INSPIRE ACTION

"Remember, the talking about the thing isn't the thing.
Doing the thing is the thing."

—AMY POEHLER

TAKING ACTION ENCOMPASSES not only *doing* but taking risks. So many aspects of our lives require risks, both big and small. Whether it's standing up for what we believe in, being true to ourselves, trying something new, or following our dreams, they all require some action and risk-taking. You will find that these mantras serve as a guide for when the going gets tough and you'd rather take the easy road. Words of encouragement help us all take a leap of faith. They build up your confidence and risk-taking repertoire one thought at a time.

"Be not afraid of going slowly;
be only afraid of standing still."

—CHINESE PROVERB

THERE COMES A moment when deliberation is no longer helpful. Thinking and planning are valuable, but there's no replacement for actually *doing* whatever you've got your sights set on. Technically, things get accomplished in a series of small steps. Don't let goals of grandeur overwhelm you; just make *some* kind of move toward your goal, even if it's a baby step. Otherwise, you may get stuck in the mud of your self-defeating statements and halting questions like: *Where do I start? There is just too much to do to make it happen. I don't have time to do it. How can I be successful at this? What if I fail? What if I embarrass myself? What if it turns out to be a mistake? I can't do this.* You get the picture.

We've all faced a major project, such as writing an essay or memoir, remodeling a house, sorting through a cluttered basement, or changing careers. The enormity of it can send us into a tailspin, and that's when we do things like binge-watch a Netflix series or doom scroll on social media. Ann Lamott wrote a fantastic book on this very subject geared toward writers entitled *Bird by Bird*. It refers to a time when her younger brother was a student stuck trying to write a report on birds. Her father inspired him by suggesting that he just needed to pick one bird to start writing about first, and then the whole report would begin to unfold "bird by bird." A great alternate mantra!

∼

So why do we spend so much time hesitating or prolonging the moment before we get started on an endeavor, an adventure, or a project? It's all about the F word. Not that F word! We're talking about *fear*. Fear of the unknown, uncertainty, failure, or rejection. Fear is a shitbag and will easily hold you back if you let it. There is a fabulous book on this topic entitled *Feel the Fear . . . and Do It Anyway* by Susan Jeffers, PhD. Jeffers writes that everyone must *accept that fear is a simple fact of life*. It's just always there. She refers to the fears that hold us back as "inner state of mind" fears. They whisper to us in the back of our minds and wreak havoc on our self-confidence. Jeffers encourages us to acknowledge our fear. In doing so, we are taking away some of its power. Next, you just have to give it the middle finger, plunge in, and do what you are afraid to do. Even a small step is great exposure therapy, and you will get a boost to your self-esteem.

> **Shout it out:**
> *Just don't stand still!*

✳ Beth ✳

When I finished graduate school, I found myself in the unique position of being without a job, with some money saved and time to travel. My favorite pastime! Unfortunately, my usual travel companions were not in the same situation. There I was for the first time, with the means and freedom to travel and nobody available to accompany me on an adventure. I was on the fence about whether to go or stay when I stumbled upon Mark Twain's quote: "Twenty years from now you will be more disappointed by the things you didn't do than by the ones you did do. So throw off the bowlines. Sail away from safe harbor. Catch the trade winds in your sails. Explore. Dream. Discover!"

The quote was a deal clincher for me. I wanted to be the person who could look back on their life with little or no regrets. So, I decided to take the initiative, *throw off my bowlines, catch the trade winds,* and travel alone. I had my sights set on traveling through South America, specifically Peru. Still, the thought of traveling solo through Latin America was frightening. This trip predates cell phones, which makes travel so much easier. My Spanish wasn't all that great (that's an understatement), and I was worried about being a female traveling alone, sensing that I would be an easy target for crime.

Ultimately, I took a leap of faith and committed to my dream trip. I must admit I was anxiety-ridden on my flight down to Lima as I contemplated the unknowns. But as I got closer, I thought about how I had taken a chance, planned it myself, and was making it happen. The sense of accomplishment I felt helped me be more assertive when I arrived. I reached out and made friends with people I might not have met had I been traveling with my husband or friends. To this day, I keep a picture of myself doing a handstand on the Isla del Sol on Lake Titicaca and one of me standing in front of Machu Picchu at sunrise to remind myself that *I am that person* who faced her fears of traveling alone. I have zero regrets about the trip. Beneath one picture, I wrote the words *Feel the Fear and Do It Anyway!* Under the other photo, I placed the Mark Twain quote. Looking at those photos still inspires me today!

~

Let's talk about ways to support and encourage goal setting.

- You are more likely to attain your goals if you **write them down**.
  My overall goal is to improve my mood and well-being.

- Break down your large project into doable tasks or **attainable** goals. No overwhelming items are allowed on your list. Then, you can cross them off when you accomplish them, preferably with a large red marker.
  I will begin a gratitude journal.

- The written goal must be **specific**, not general or vague. Your goal must also be **measurable** and **time-related**.
  I will write at least three things that went well, I am proud of, or I am grateful for in my life. I will do this every night for one week.

- Think about what you are getting from the goal or how it is **relevant**.
  This gratitude journal will increase my joy in life and my positive thoughts. I may even use it as a jumping-off point to start an online blog about mindfulness and healthy living.

These are known as SMART goals—specific, measurable, achievable, relevant, and time-bound. When you start using these, you'll see a difference in making progress toward your goals. Too often, we trip ourselves up from taking a single action step because it all seems so overwhelming. Go ahead and take that first step; whether a giant leap or a teeny tiny one, any forward movement is a win. The pride and satisfaction you will derive from taking these actionable steps is invigorating. Going slowly is nothing to worry about . . . just don't stand still!

✶ **It's Your Turn to Play, Explore, and Learn** ✶

Fucking Do It Anyway

This exercise is about facing your fears in combination with a goal. What is something you've been wanting to do but fear is holding you back? It can be a little thing or a whopper. For example, *I've been afraid to go out and explore new social groups because it will be uncomfortable.* Or *I'm afraid to quit smoking because it's a habit, and I depend on it for distraction.* Then, set a small goal (how about a SMART one?) about your topic. The social topic could be *I'm going to check out groups on meetup.com to see if there's something I'd be interested in by tomorrow.* For smoking, it could be, *I am going to make an appointment with my primary care doctor to discuss prescription options.* After you meet the goal, set a new one to keep the momentum going. Even though these changes involve some level of fear, you are one step closer to fucking doing them anyway!

✷ Quotes That Support This Mantra and Inspire ✷

- "You miss 100% of the shots you don't take."
  —Wayne Gretzky

- "It's not about standing still and becoming safe. If anybody wants to keep creating they have to be about change."
  —Miles Davis

- "Talk doesn't cook rice."
  —Chinese Proverb

- "The dread of doing a task uses up more time and energy than doing the task itself."
  —Rita Emmett

- "Just keep swimming."
  —Dory from *Finding Nemo*

✷ Alternate Mantra Ideas for This Topic ✷

- *Bird by Bird*—Ann Lamott

- Feel the fear and do it anyway, damn it!

- Baby Steps—*What About Bob?* (1991)

- Act or accept.

✷ Songs to Add to Your Just Don't Stand Still Playlist ✷

- "A Little Less Conversation"
    by Elvis Presley

- "Chances"
    by Blake Shelton

- "Flashdance . . . What a Feeling"
    by Irene Cara

- "Our Lives"
    by The Calling

- "Jump Right In"
    by Zac Brown Band

✷ Further Resources ✷

- *Atomic Habits: An Easy & Proven Way to Build Good Habits & Break Bad Ones*
    by James Clear

- *Get Off Your "But": How to End Self-Sabotage and Stand Up for Yourself*
    by Sean Stephenson

- *Monday Morning Motivation: Inspirational Messages That Motivate You to Start Your Week Off Right*
    by Monica Marie Jones

- *The Magic Lamp: Goal Setting for People Who Hate Setting Goals* by Keith Ellis

"Through meditation and by giving full attention to one thing at a time, we can learn to direct attention where we choose."
—Eknath Easwaran

PHILOSOPHERS, RELIGIONS, AND spiritual leaders have collaborated on the benefits of living mindfully for a *long* time. The overall consensus is that learning how to be in the moment enriches your quality of life, makes it more meaningful, and allows you to experience it more fully. The past and future only exist in our minds. That's not to say you should never remember the past or plan for the future again, but focusing on them too much heightens rumination, ramps up anxiety, and steals joy from the present. A hilarious scene in the movie *I Heart Huckabees* portrays the challenges associated with staying in the present moment. We encourage you to watch the movie or check out the clip on YouTube! Mark Wahlberg and Jason Schwartzman are practicing mindfulness by slamming each other in the face with a ball, yelling, "Now!" Their instructor points out to them that they cannot stay in the here and now all day because it is inevitable that they will be drawn back into human drama, suffering, and desires.

Mark Wahlberg says, "So we get drawn back into human drama and how important we think that is. Then we do crazy stuff. We have to go back to the ball." Yep, that's the way it works!

A Harvard University study by Matthew A. Killingsworth and Daniel T. Gilbert concluded that our level of happiness is very much related to how much our minds wander. The more engaged we are in whatever we do, the higher our satisfaction levels tend to be. To clarify, mindfulness is not about obliterating all thoughts. The idea is to acknowledge them and picture them rolling on by. This creates that marvelous detachment where you can choose whether you want to buy into your thoughts or let them go. One of our favorite ways to practice mindfulness, well, other than the *I Heart Huckabees* method of slamming a ball in our face, is through meditation. There are different kinds of meditation, but they all prompt you to focus on the present and *leave your mind behind*. After you've practiced for a while, you'll be more likely to detach from strong emotions and thoughts in your everyday life and let them dissipate before reacting. Imagine your child screaming, "I hate you!" That brings up some powerful thoughts and feelings, right? If you can pause instead of immediately reacting, you open up the possibility of handling a stressful situation in a more productive and healthy way.

Meditation conjures up images of the lotus position, incense, and Buddhist monks chanting in the background, right? That's one way to do it. But meditation isn't limited to certain positions or activities. It's whatever relaxes you, prompts you to slow down, and puts you in "the zone." It can be as simple as taking a twenty-second pause every hour, acknowledging what your senses are taking in, focusing on your breath, and most importantly, not trying to control anything, figure anything out, or make anything happen. As we've mentioned, we get locked into control mode because our limbic system is wired for survival and wants to make sure we are safe. It's constantly scanning for danger, thinking about what to do next and how to make things happen. This primitive part of our brain is all fear-based. In today's day and age, the fear of not setting up shelter before nightfall or running into sabertooth tigers is not really a big thing here. So, we end up focusing on controlling emotional fears, such as the fear of emotional disconnection, failure, or not being enough the way we are. Unfortunately, this need for control turns our attention away from the present moment. We get caught up in changing things from the way they are, leading to hesitation, tension, and anxiety. This preoccupation can cause a small feeling of uneasiness or something more intense, like dread or panic. We get so involved with directing our lives that we forget to be curious and present. Remember, our inner dialogue is what creates our reality, and awareness is the key to breaking this cycle. So, stop listening to your crazy-ass thoughts and work on accepting each moment. Some even call this a sacred pause. We have been practicing these sacred pauses and found it to be an absolute game-changer. What a difference a small moment of stillness in our minds can make!

Meditation extends to any activity that helps you let go, such as being in nature, gardening, drawing, listening to music, knitting, swimming, or biking, as long as you are mindful of where you are and what you are doing. It is also a form of grounding, a self-soothing technique that calms your brain down by getting out of your head and focusing on the here and now. Just walking can be meditative if you pay attention. Focus on the motion of putting one foot in front of the other, your breath, the fresh air, colors, and sounds of nature. This is called active meditation. It's an accessible, affordable way to quiet the chatter in your mind and focus on the present. Leaving your mind behind encourages us to have a to-be list instead of a to-do list. For example, be mindful, aware, present, in the moment, curious, or still. A visualization that works wonderfully is imagining yourself without a head. All that chatter is reduced to nothing. Just be.

We know you have a boatload of things going on in your mind; we all do. Gone are the days when you unplugged, with no social media, texts, emails, or streamed shows to catch up on. The to-do lists and distractions of today would have been inconceivable fifty years ago. These days, sitting on a porch with iced tea and doing nothing is a luxury, not a typical evening! In fact, it goes against our current social norms.

Consequently, many of us get anxious by even thinking about the idea of stillness. We're here to tell you that slowing down and being in the moment is incredibly good for you. Remember, the past and future exist only in your mind. When you're focused on them, the actual moment you're experiencing is clouded with shadows and noise.

That's why your dog is always happy. He lives in the moment. Does this mean you should never think or multitask again? Heck no! That's not even possible. But if you consciously take time to be present at least once a day, you'll notice a positive difference in your overall outlook. Be conscious of your breath, senses, body, and surroundings, and even chores can become more peaceful. Take folding laundry—feel the texture of the fabrics, smell the detergent, be aware of your body, take deep breaths, and voilà! You're doing active meditation.

Try some of the different meditation styles in the exercises below and see if you find one that helps you bring your attention to the present. There are also plenty of meditation apps, YouTube videos, and audio guides if you'd like some additional structure to start you off. Just a few minutes of meditation can reduce your resting heart rate, blood pressure, and negative emotions. It encourages acceptance and increases patience and tolerance. The more you practice, the more you'll cultivate the habit of being present in all that you do.

✶ It's Your Turn to Play, Explore, and Learn ✶

Mindful Meditation

- This is basic, nothing fancy. Start by focusing on your breath; when thoughts come up, notice them and let them go without judgment. When your mind wanders, bring your attention back to your breath and the present moment. You'll probably start thinking, *I'm not doing this right* within five seconds of starting. Not to worry—that's the brain doing its thing, constantly chattering and making shit up.

- You can turn this into active meditation by finding a soothing activity such as walking, yoga, gardening, tai chi, fixing your stereo, drinking coffee, whatever! Simply *do it while noticing*.

- Try picking a calming word, mantra, or sound, and repeat it to yourself. For example, "Letting go, letting go, letting go." This will cut down on the inevitable distractions from your brain. This type of meditation is prominent in Hindu and Buddhist teachings. Many of them use the sound "aum" because it is said to be the same vibrational frequency of everything in nature. When you chant it, you acknowledge your connectedness to nature and every living thing. Chanting slows down the nervous system and relaxes the body.

> **Breathe in and repeat,**
> *Leave your mind behind.*

Visualization

- Visualization is a powerful meditation technique elite athletes use to gain self-confidence, calm anxiety, declutter the mind, boost motivation, and improve mood. They simply visualize themselves performing their best. Try meditating by seeing yourself fantastically handling things related to your future goals. For example, if you are working on overeating, watch yourself going through the day. Be aware of your triggers and work toward consistently making more healthy food choices.

- Another meditative visualization technique is to create a safe place that is comforting for you. This facilitates the relaxation response in your body. It's perfect for calming you down when negative thoughts are closing in and your system is about to wig out. It's kind of like in *Office Space,* where Peter Gibbons asks his therapist if he can just hypnotize him, so all day, when he's really working, he thinks he's fishing. Visualization lets you take that fishing trip in your mind. So you're going to conjure up a place like the beach, a lake, the forest, or a bench in the park. Again, when you involve all your senses, it will be much more effective. So instead of just "the beach," try something like this: You are sitting on the beach. There's no one else around. You can smell the salty air, feel the sun on your skin and the warm sand between your toes, hear the crashing waves and seagulls cry, taste the cold drink you brought with you, and see a few tiny boats in the distance.

Progressive Muscle Relaxation (PMR)

This meditative experience is great for managing the effects of stress, tension, and anxiety. It's beneficial for high blood pressure, chronic pain, and sleep issues. PMR is based on the theory that physical relaxation promotes mental relaxation. We already know the mind and body are thicker than thieves, so this makes sense. The idea is to tense each muscle group, although not to the point of strain, for five to ten seconds. Then, you notice how it feels when you relax the muscles for ten to twenty seconds. There are lots of YouTube videos and apps that have guided PMR. Here's an example to give you the idea:

- Start by taking five deep, slow breaths in through your nose and out through your mouth.

- Clench your fists and tighten your muscles all the way up your arm as hard as you can without straining. Hold a little longer than you think you can. And release. Notice how relaxed and fluid your hands and arms feel.

- Tense your leg muscles. Pay attention to the tension. Continue taking deep, slow breaths while you are holding the muscles tightly, and count to ten. And release. Notice the difference when you let go.

- Continue doing the same process for all the major muscles of your body, such as your calves, buttocks, shoulders, face, and any other areas where you feel tension.

- Lastly, tense everything up in your whole body. Hold, hold, and hold! Then, release along with a slow exhale of breath. Notice how free and flexible you feel. Take a big stretch and let your body go limp.

✻ Inspirational Quotes That Support This Mantra ✻

- "Life is a dance. Mindfulness is witnessing that dance."
    —Amit Ray

- "Today is a gift. That's why we call it the present."
    —Eleanor Roosevelt

- " . . . the meeting of two eternities, the past and the future, which is precisely the present moment . . ."
    —Henry David Thoreau

- "The past exists only in our memories, the future only in our plans. The present is our only reality."
    —Robert M. Pirsig

- "You can clutch the past so tightly to your chest that it leaves your arms too full to embrace the present."
  —Jan Gildewell

✳ Alternate Mantras for This Mantra ✳

- Release the past and seize the present.

- Notice, notice, notice!

- The present is here! Make the most of it.

- The past is a guidepost, not a hitching post.

- Be present.

✳ Songs to Add to Your Meditation Playlist ✳

- "Do You Realize??"
  by The Flaming Lips

- "Good Ole Days"
  by Macklemore, featuring Kesha

- "Hey Hey Hey"
  by Michael Franti & Spearhead

- "Live Like You Were Dying"
  by Tim McGraw

- "Secret o' Life"
  by James Taylor

✳ Further Resources ✳

- *A Mindfulness Guide for the Frazzled*
  by Ruby Wax

- *Altered Traits: Science Reveals How Meditation Changes Your Mind, Brain, and Body*
  by Daniel Goleman and Richard J. Davidson

- *Five Minute Meditation: Mindfulness, Stress Relief, and Focus for Absolute Beginners*
    by Lisa Shea

- *Forest Bathing: How Trees Can Help You Find Health and Happiness*
    by Dr. Qing Li

- *Full Catastrophe Living: Using the Wisdom of Your Body and Mind to Face, Stress, Pain, and Illness*
    by Jon Kabat-Zinn

- *The Power of Now: A Spiritual Guide to Enlightenment*
    by Eckhart Tolle

- *The Things You Can See Only When You Slow Down: How to Be Calm in a Busy World*
    by Haemin Sun

"When you focus on the good, the good gets better."
—Esther Hicks

Martin Seligman began the *positive psychology movement* in 1997, which changed the focus of psychology from studying dysfunction to learning more about the things that make life worth living. Since then, there's been tons of research on this and what they call positive psychology interventions or PPIs for cool acronym slingers like us! One of the most successful and heavily researched PPIs is none other than gratitude. Gratitude tunes your heart and mind into positive things you've had all along but fail to appreciate. It is so simple, yet practicing gratitude consistently shows an increase in the overall quality of life. It's amazing what happens when we focus on and appreciate what is already there. We just have to practice paying attention.

Practicing gratitude on a regular basis changes your brain. It increases the feel-good chemicals we love, such as serotonin and dopamine, contributing to your sense of fulfillment and calmness. So, it acts like a natural antidepressant. It's also been proven to boost your immune system and help you sleep better. Gratitude increases the neuron density and gray matter in your brain, giving your prefrontal cortex a boost! With that extra brain power, you'll be able to notice *more* good things in your life. In other words, once you start practicing gratitude, the effect multiplies. The bonus side effect is while your prefrontal cortex increases in size, your amygdala shrinks. Remember, the amygdala is that little asshole that triggers feelings of anxiety and the fight-flight-freeze response.

A thinking trap many of us fall into is waiting to begin appreciating our lives until we hit a particular mile marker. For example, I'll be happier when the kids are out of the house, I retire, I lose weight, I finish those projects around the house, I meet someone new, I have more money, *when . . . , when . . . , when*! Unfortunately, there is no point in life where you arrive and all your struggles evaporate. They're part of the journey. The spiritual leader Alfred D. Souza has a great thought on this: "For a long time, it had seemed to me that life was about to begin—real life. But there were always some obstacles in the way, something to be gotten through first, some unfinished business, time still to be served, and a debt to be paid. Then life would begin. At last, it dawned on me that these obstacles were my life." What a fabulous sentiment encouraging us to embrace obstacles as a given in life and find happiness along the journey.

If you like country music, we highly recommend two songs along this vein. The first one is "You're Gonna Miss This" by Trace Adkins. It simultaneously increases awareness that time only passes by once and reminds us to find gratitude as well. It's about a young woman who can't wait to get to the next stage of her life. For example, when she's in high school, she wants to move out, and when she's married and living in an apartment, she can't wait for kids and a house, and so on. Different people in her life tell her to slow down:

> *You're gonna miss this*
> *You're gonna want this back*

You're gonna wish these days hadn't gone by so fast
These are some good times
So take a good look around
You may not know it now
But you're gonna miss this

These lyrics encourage us to focus on the good stuff in our life instead of continually looking to the future. The second song is "It Won't Be Like This for Long" by Darius Rucker. This song particularly relates to appreciating the stages and ages of children. A family is raising a new baby and uses the phrase *it won't be like this for long* related to each new stage, such as crying all night, refusing to let you leave at preschool, and saying they hate you as a teenager. We are both parents and have used the *It won't be like this for long* mantra to remind us to appreciate the kiddos at each stage because it will all fly by too fast.

> **Close your eyes and repeat,**
> *Focus on the good (right now!).*

✷ Helene ✷

I OFTEN GET stuck in a control mode and want to figure things out and get my shit together before I can enjoy life. I want to have all my wisdom color coded and in little file folders. Then, I will take a deep sigh of relief. At that moment, my life will *truly begin* because *I know what I'm doing*. I will be free to experience my journey as an enlightened, centered person who never feels lost or empty. Game on. I'll be ready to be the perfect wife, mother, daughter, friend, and therapist. No more detours, self-destructive behaviors, or fuck ups. As you can guess, that moment never happened. I did figure out that such a moment is not *going* to happen. Resigning myself to the concept that change and ambiguity are constant in life has resulted in a newfound sense of freedom. It helps me to stop thinking about reaching that point where I am ultimately fulfilled, and it encourages me to practice finding comfort and contentment in each moment as it is. Uncertainties included! Perhaps there are no set answers except the ones we come up with within ourselves, and even those will deepen, shift, and develop further with time. I've since chosen to favor this quote from the actor and writer Nick Frost: "I am a work in progress, and I hope I'll never be complete." Because if I'm complete, it means I'm six feet under.

$\sim$

Our society tells us what to appreciate and what not to appreciate. This pattern has been going on for years. This cultural power is imposed upon us without choice by marketing and media. We get trapped in the same thoughts and behaviors just because culture dictates it, whether it makes us genuinely happy or not. In today's culture, a screwed-up phenomenon is searching for happiness through external means—buying cars, clothes, and gadgets. Do these things really make us happy? Perhaps temporarily, and that's all right. However, they do not meet the innate needs that things cannot buy. Gary Zukav and Linda Francis, authors of *The Heart of the Soul: Emotional Awareness*, say, "The need to feel safe, valuable, and loved is at the core of the human experience." They believe the plight of attaining these things externally has overtaken society.

Material goods are not bad in themselves; it is the way they're used that's harmful. Constantly looking outside of ourselves and our relationships to find "enoughness" is a recipe for a high credit card balance and stuff we probably don't need. Our society will always sell and buy more goods than we ever truly need. Becoming cognizant that these things are not the core of ourselves but a far-off extension is worthwhile. Living simply is not about giving up all your materials like your car or house, buying secondhand clothing, or growing your own food, although there is merit in all those things. It's about acknowledging the root elements that truly affect your quality of life. So, enjoy the good things in life that you love and have a passion for, but know that you don't need these things to be happy. As with everything, *look for a balance*. Use your mantras to prompt gratitude for what is already there, and you'll find more satisfaction.

An attitude of gratitude often washes over us in the wake of a crisis. Traumatic events cause us to take a step back and realize what is truly important in life, followed by a greater appreciation for these things. This phenomenon also happens with individuals who have near-death experiences. They are said to be happier than others because they take less for granted. After the September 11 attacks in the US, attendance at simple living seminars skyrocketed. Similar happenings occurred again relating to the doomsday predictions of the Mayan calendar ending on December 21, 2012, and the COVID-19 pandemic. What does this tell us? Many people started to slow down and notice the simple things, like safety, security, and quality time with loved ones. When things are status quo, we *all* get complacent with what we have, and we expect it always to be there. Nobody is immune from this. But with a little gratitude, we can magnify all the important things in our lives and let the rest go.

※ **It's Your Turn to Play, Explore, and Learn** ※

Gratitude Journaling

Gratitude journaling is impossible to fuck up. Simply jot down a few things you enjoyed, went well, or are thankful for each day. We've listed further expansion prompts for those of you who like to write! There are also crazy good apps for your phone, which makes it handy to practice gratitude when you're in line at the grocery store or waiting at a doctor's office.

- List ways to share your gratitude today with other peeps in your life.

- What abilities, strengths, and traits are you glad you have?

- What activities would you miss if you couldn't do them anymore?

- What stuff do you take for granted in your life? Be specific, such as running water, electricity, your urinary system, or your car starting.

- Who in your life (animals count, of course) are you thankful for? Express what you are grateful for about them.

- What aspects of your environment and nature are you thankful for?

- Draw some good moments from your day. Have fun with it!

Talisman

Select a rock or an object that you like. Put it somewhere you'll see it every day, like in your car or by the coffee maker. A necklace or other piece of jewelry works as well. Whenever you see or feel it in your hand, think of something that brings you joy or you are grateful for. This talisman will be your secret mindfulness weapon. As you know, we need as many reminders as we can to insert those positive thoughts!

A variation of the talisman is a worry stone. This is an ancient tradition utilized by many cultures throughout history. Simply find a smooth stone in nature or purchase a polished stone if you prefer. The concept of a worry stone is to physically unburden our worries and fears by rubbing them into the stone. This simple symbolic gesture encourages relaxation and letting go. It acts as a mindful meditation encouraging you to rub away your stress, uneasiness, and doubts.

Random Acts of Kindness

Practicing random acts of kindness has many of the same effects as gratitude. Plus, it gets you into the moment. It doesn't have to be anything big—help someone with their groceries, smile, open the door for someone, actively listen to a friend's problems, compliment a coworker, whatever! Sonja Lyubomirsky, researcher and author of *The Myths of Happiness: What Should Make You Happy, but Doesn't,*

What Shouldn't Make You Happy, but Does, conducted a six-week study on this topic. Participants who performed five acts of kindness every week for six weeks reported an increase in happiness. Our favorite feel-good chemicals are released because we have better self-esteem and positive social connections when we're doing nice stuff. Who doesn't need more of that? The study also showed that mixing up the type of kindness you perform keeps it fresh and fun. Pick up litter one day and make someone laugh the next! Kindness doesn't cost anything and is available to us twenty-four seven. Jot your random acts of kindness down in your journal to encourage accountability and mindfulness.

✷ Inspirational Quotes that Support This Mantra ✷

- "Enjoy the little things, for one day you may look back and realize they were the big things."
  —Robert Brault

- "It's a funny thing about life, once you begin to take note of the things you are grateful for, you begin to lose sight of the things that you lack."
  —Germany Kent

- "In ordinary life, we hardly realize that we receive a great deal more than we give and that it is only with gratitude that life becomes rich."
  —Dietrich Bonhoeffer

- "What separates privilege from entitlement is gratitude."
  —Brené Brown

- "The more grateful I am, the more beauty I see."
  —Mary Davis

✷ Alternate Mantra Ideas for This Topic ✷

- Notice the shit right in front of you.

- Enjoy every step, even the missteps.
- Happiness is a way of travel.
- Practice an attitude of gratitude.
- You're gonna miss this.

✶ Songs to Add to Your Gratitude Playlist ✶

- "Getting Good"
  by Lauren Alaina

- "You're Gonna Miss This"
  by Trace Adkins

- "100 Years"
  by Five for Fighting

- "Tell Me Something Good"
  by Rufus & Chaka Khan

- "It Won't Be Like This for Long"
  by Darius Rucker

✶ Further Resources ✶

- *The Simple Living Guide: A Source for Less Stressful, More Joyful Living*
  by Janet Luhrs

- *Focus on the Good Stuff: The Power of Appreciation*
  by Mike Robbins

- *Thanks!: How the New Science of Gratitude Can Make You Happier*
  by Robert A. Emmons

- *The Psychology of Gratitude*
  by Robert A. Emmons and Michael E. McCullough

- *A Simple Act of Gratitude: How Learning to Say Thank You Changed My Life*
    by John Kralik

- *The Gratitude Diaries: How a Year Looking on the Bright Side Can Transform Your Life*
    by Janice Kaplan

- The Science of Gratitude—YouTube

Sticky Note Mantras

Mix It Up

"I love to mix it up. I love to keep doing different things."
—Clive Owen

MIXING IT UP is all about balancing your life with different activities to spur growth, stimulation, and inspiration. We are all complex, multifaceted, and multidimensional creatures. The mind, body, and spirit thrive on mixing it up! Add in a dash of mindfulness, and you'll be able to consciously feed all aspects of your physical, spiritual, emotional, sexual, and intellectual sides. Each element of the self is connected to another element, affecting the whole kit and caboodle.

We all tend to focus on specific aspects of ourselves, such as appearance, hobbies, career, or family, which is okay. However, becoming conscious of the realms we shy away from prompts us to learn, grow, and find meaning. These neglected realms are the exact pieces of yourself you should focus on when it's time to *mix it up*. For instance, most of us have used the "I've got no time to exercise and eat healthy cause I'm too fucking busy" excuse at one time or another. Yeah, the struggle is real. But if you make time to nurture the physical part of yourself, everything else you do will be with renewed vitality. Your body will thank you, and your spirit will feel lighter. Here's a great visual called the Life Balance Wheel to help you out in assessing the equilibrium of different aspects of your life. If you divided this pie chart to represent your life, the pieces

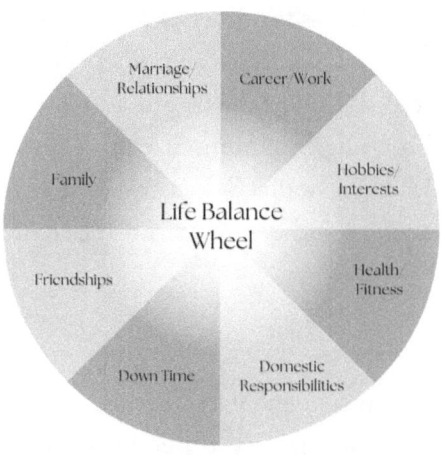

of the pie would certainly not be equal. Our time and energy get distributed more thickly in some areas, and others are spread thin. You don't have to necessarily upend your life and start training for a marathon or buy a sailboat; start with some micro movements toward change. See the exercises at the end for further expansion on the life balance wheel.

✻ Helene ✻

BEING THE ANALYTICAL type, I always get stuck in my head. I call this "getting in a funk." When I'm in a funk, I get caught in an unproductive, analytical, revolving thought process, *and I can't turn my brain off!* My husband knows me so well —when I'm spinning my wheels and overthinking, he'll come up to me and say, "I sense a disturbance in the force." What is it with guys and *Star Wars*? Sometimes, we'll discuss the issue I am wrestling with, and this interaction helps me. Most of the time, I just need to get out of my own head for a while and do something completely different. I have been known to get into funks frequently while I am writing. In fact, this section right here is pissing me off! Just kidding. Glued to the computer screen and intent on finishing a section, I'll obsess over it and keep writing and rewriting. My inner critic creeps into my head, saying *it's not good enough and will never be good enough*. Then, my wise counselor (I always picture my dog—she's so wise) steps up and tells me to *mix it up!* So I'll take a break, which shakes up my perspective and refreshes my spirit. I have found it helps me to put a time limit on my computer work. It's like browsing the internet; you sit down and then look at the clock, and it's been hours! When my time is up, I know it's time to change my activity and be present for different experiences.

~

If you struggle with turning your brain off like Helene, try different activities when you are wound up and find something that's therapeutic for you. Remember to really *be there* in the moment. After crawling out of your own head for a while, your mind will be in a different place and process information through an altered set of lenses. Carl Rogers comments on the importance of *mixing it up* in his amazing book, *A Way of Being:*

> It is necessary for me to stay close to the earthiness of real experience. I cannot live my life in abstractions. So real relationships, hands dirtied in the soil, observing the budding flower, or viewing the sunset, are necessary to my life. At least one foot must be in the soil of reality. . . . I like my life best when it faces outward most of the time. I prize the times when I am inward-looking—searching to know myself, meditating, and thinking. But this must be balanced by doing things—interacting with people, producing something, whether a flower or a book or a piece of carpentry.

Taking time to be present and involving ourselves in activities that fully captivate our attention has been found to contribute enormously to overall happiness. Theorist Mihaly Csikszentmihalyi has named being fully involved in the moment as the state of "flow." You've probably heard the adage that time flies when you're having fun. That's what happens when you're in the state of flow. You lose track of time and, more importantly, yourself.

Mixing it up also means getting out of your comfort zone. Adventure doesn't have to mean a trip to Italy; it's simply being open to trying new things. Applying the attitude of adventure to your daily life shifts your mindset, adding new energy and purpose. So be conscious of always choosing to play it safe. You may have to manage a little anxiety, but a little exposure therapy is good for you! Take on a challenge at work, go to a new restaurant, make an unfamiliar recipe, sign up for a yoga class, meet your neighbor, etc. Bigger adventures can also have a profound effect on your outlook. Think of something you've always wanted to try, such as salsa dancing, zip lining, knitting, exploring the country, volunteering, goat yoga, learning to play an instrument, or tai chi. Honestly, you're not going to remember the times you emptied the dishwasher or sat at the computer. Picking just one activity every month or two adds novelty to your life, challenges you, and spices things up. You'll look forward to it, and the positive feelings will stay with you long after your adventure.

A word of caution for you newly converted dare-doers: things will not always work out the way we imagine. But if we never take a chance, we'll miss out on a whole lot of enrichment and growth. While we sure as heck don't always get a say in our experiences or how they turn out, just being open to learning through any new path creates an opportunity. It's an opportunity to rock a whole different side of yourself.

Mixing it up also involves taking stock of the time we spend with others versus the time we spend alone. We are all on the spectrum from introverts to extroverts; some of us reboot by being alone, and others recharge by being with others. That makes sense since we are all unique individuals, but it takes a toll on our mental health if we are too lopsided. These days, more and more people are spending time alone and feeling disconnected from others. In fact, loneliness is at an all-time high in the United States. The surgeon general's advisory in 2023 indicated half of Americans reported feeling lonely, and only 40 percent said they felt connected to others. The advisory also reports that the effects of social isolation on our physical health are equivalent to smoking up to fifteen cigarettes a day. It puts us at a higher risk of heart disease, stroke, anxiety, depression, and dementia. Loneliness increases mortality rates by over 20 percent in all species, even fruit flies!

> **Remember and repeat,**
> *Mix it the fuck up!*

Loneliness isn't limited to people who have no friends or acquaintances. You can have many friends, coworkers, and social engagements and still feel lonely. Carl Jung, the Swiss psychiatrist and psychoanalyst, agrees: "Loneliness does not come from having no people around you, but from being unable to communicate the things that seem important to you." Even if you're married, you can feel lonely if you aren't connecting with your partner. It takes five positive interactions for every negative or emotionally charged interaction to keep the relationship healthy and rewarding. So, we need those positive interchanges to feel connected. We're sure you have seen families having dinner together at a restaurant, but they're all typing away on their phones, probably on social media. In theory, social media connects us, but does it really? Connecting through technology may have merit, but not when it means we're missing out on the connections we can experience in real life.

It is also essential to recognize which of our relationships are reciprocal. In any relationship, there is give and take, but when one side is not trying, it is not a healthy relationship. Those people who are unsupportive, treat you poorly, or are social underminers are detrimental to your sense of belonging. Avoid those relationships like the Spanish flu! Cultivate meaningful relationships, the ones that challenge you, comfort you, energize you, and help you grow. Hang onto them when you find them because they are a beautiful thing!

✳ It's Your Turn to Play, Explore, and Learn ✳

Keep It in Balance

Take a look at the life balance wheel and reflect on each piece of the pie. Here are some questions to get you started:

- Do I make an effort to spend time alone?

- Do I take time to interact with others?

- Do I nurture the physical side of myself?

- Do I take time to nurture my mind and reflect?

- Do I take time to just *be* and enjoy experiences?

- Do I spend time connecting with my spiritual self in some way?

- Do I take risks and involve myself in aspects of life I am uncomfortable with?

Take Stock of Your Risk-Taking

We've all taken risks to get where we are today. That's how we learn new skills and improve, right? Reflect on your life in regard to risk-taking and all the good things that came of it. Whether it was playing chess, dancing, parenting, using the computer, playing an instrument, participating in a sport, or learning how to excel in your job, what are some risk-taking endeavors you are glad about now? What would you still like to do?

✳ Inspirational Quotes That Support This Mantra ✳

- "One hour of life, crowded to the full with glorious action, and filled with noble risks, is worth whole years of those mean observances of paltry decorum, in which men steal through existence, like sluggish waters through a marsh, without either honour or observation."
  —Walter Scott

- "It is only in adventure that some people succeed in knowing themselves—in finding themselves."
  —Andre Gide

- "There is only one map to the journey of life and it lives within your heart."
  —Willie Nelson

- "If you play it safe in life, you've decided you don't want to grow anymore."
  —Shirley Hufstedler

✳ Alternate Mantra Ideas for This Topic ✳

- My comfort zone may be getting too comfy.

- It's now or never.

- Time to shake things up!

- Change is where growth happens.

✳ Songs to Add to Your Mix It Up Playlist ✳

- "Standing Outside the Fire"
  by Garth Brooks

- "Break Away"
  by Rascal Flatts

- "I Take My Chances"
    by Mary Chapin Carpenter

- "It's My Life"
    by Bon Jovi

- "Live Like You Were Dying"
    by Tim McGraw

✳ Further Resources ✳

- *Change or Die: The Three Keys to Change at Work and in Life*
    by Alan Deutschman

- *Flow: The Psychology of Optimal Experience*
    by Mihaly Csikszentmihalyi

- *Transitions: Making Sense of Life's Changes*
    by William Bridges

- *Under The Tuscan Sun*
    by Frances Mayes

- *100 Ways to Motivate Yourself: Change Your Life Forever*
    by Steve Chandler

Mantras About Self-care

STICKY NOTE MANTRAS

"Your phone needs to recharge every night. Your laptop needs to recharge. Everything needs to recharge. Are you giving yourself space, time, and effort to recharge?"

—Jay Shetty

SELF-CARE IS a buzzword these days, and for good reason! Today's society is busier than ever, and we need to make it a priority to take some time out to recharge. Seriously, we have a biological need for rest and play. However, that balance can get out of whack and pretty lopsided! After all, "All work and no play makes Jack a dull boy."

And when we take the time for self-care, we do everything else in our lives better! Aspects of recharging look slightly different for everyone, but some universal concepts affect us all. For instance, almost everyone needs to make time for connections with others, introspection, eating healthy and exercising, and our all-time favorite, relaxation.

```
All work and no play makes Jack a dull boy.
All work and no play makes Jack a dull boy.
All work and no play makes Jack a dull boy.
All work and no play makes Jack a dull boy.
All work and no play makes Jack a dull boy.
All work and no play makes Jack a dull boy.
All work and no play makes Jack a dull boy.
All work and no play makes Jack a dull boy.
```

The Shining, Steven King

"Almost everything will work again if you unplug it
for a few minutes, including you."
—Anne Lamott

BRAVERY, CHANGE, AND trying different things to inspire growth isn't easy. We know this. We have tried everything in this book too. Some days, implementing these ideas comes easy, and some days, we must dig a little deeper, make course corrections, or take a mulligan and try again later. One thing is for sure: it is a hell of a lot easier when you don't feel like shit. That's where self-care comes in. When we exercise, eat right, sleep, and are intellectually stimulated, grateful, and connected to our community, it makes us ready for, you know, life. Your mind, body, spirit, and soul need nurturing to function on a daily basis and facilitate the changes and growth you are trying to accomplish. In other words, you have to take care of yourself, peeps!

Self-care is consciously choosing to do things to better your overall physical and mental well-being. They aren't always fun, but you know they are good for you! For example, getting up early to do your yoga routine so you feel more centered the rest of the day or making a financial plan to pay off debts and spend wisely. It is an intentional and thoughtful practice that asks, *Does this benefit me in the long run, or is it just giving me good feelings for the present moment?* Creating rituals for self-care is a great way to build it into your everyday routine. We need to schedule it into our day because self-care is usually the first thing to go out the window in times of added stress, dysfunction, or crisis. Ironically, that's when we need it most! We stop caring for ourselves, putting everything and everyone else first, and then crash and burn.

Think of it this way. By practicing self-care, you are actively taking a role in cultivating long-term purpose and making positive choices. It's like saying, *I'm important, and there are things I need to do for myself daily to function at my best.* Use this mantra as a cue throughout your day! As it states, self-care is not self-indulgence! Self–indulgence is distracting yourself from your problems, such as overdoing it by treating yourself, chasing those dopamine hits from instant gratification, and engaging in unhealthy coping strategies.

✲ Helene ✲

SELF-CARE IS ONE of my many challenges. I'm one of those people who takes care of everyone else, including my dogs, better than myself. This is hilarious because I'm a therapist and always preach this stuff. However, I made a commitment that if I'm able to come home from the office at lunch, I'm going to do *some sort* of physical activity. It may be walking the dogs around the block, a fifteen-minute YouTube video, or stretching out on a mat. If I can't make it home for lunch, I walk around the building several times. Even though I have chronic pain, I can usually find *something* that works. I can't tell you how much of a difference this has made for me! I put myself first, which pays off, am more present with my afternoon clients, and feel physically better too!

∼

Pressing the pause button on life is worth the time, effort, and hassle it takes to schedule self-care into your daily routines. But *you* are *so* worth it! We all are. Even with the modern conveniences we now have, we still feel more pressed for time and energy than ever. It feels like there aren't ever

enough hours in the day. Scrolling online, phone calls, and answering emails are available to us twenty-four seven. That shit takes time! We feel stretched and overwhelmed with all these demands on our time and attention. As Bilbo Baggins says in *The Hobbit*, "I feel thin, like butter spread across too much bread." This chronic feeling of being overwhelmed leads to burnout, fuzzy thinking, low motivation, and feeling stuck. Demands of us and our time are coming at us from all facets of life: work, family, relationships, media, finances, the list goes on. The simple life has gone out the window! The American Psychological Association released the following statement in a recent report: "Stress in America 2022: Concerned for the Future, Beset by Inflation, shows a battered American psyche, facing a barrage of external stressors mostly out of personal control. The survey found a majority of adults are disheartened by government and political divisiveness, daunted by historic inflation levels, and dismayed by widespread violence."

In today's busy world, it's no small wonder that we all feel pulled in many directions. To add to this stress, we also spend a lot of time worrying about things we may or may not have control over. But (there is always a but) we do have control over whether we *prioritize self-care*. Again, making it part of our everyday routine is essential because it is too easily shoved out of the way in favor of the supposed tos and have tos.

Some of you are thinking, *How in the world can I fit anything else in my life? I work, care for children and loved ones, commute, clean, cook, etc. I don't have time to go to the gym or sit down and read a book.* We're not saying it has to be excessive amounts of time each day. Small moments count! For example, take sixty seconds to breathe slowly and deeply. Calm your mind with a visual mantra. Sixty seconds, that's all. It can be that easy to press the pause button!

There's a well-known story (author unknown) about a university professor making a point about the importance of prioritizing how we spend our time:

> *A professor of philosophy stood before his class with some items in front of him. When the class began, wordlessly, he picked up a large empty mayonnaise jar and filled it with rocks about two inches in diameter.*
>
> *He then asked the students if the jar was full. They agreed that it was full. So, the professor then picked up a box of pebbles and poured them into the jar. He shook the jar lightly and watched as the pebbles rolled into the open areas between the rocks. The professor then asked the students again if the jar was full. They chuckled and agreed that it was indeed full this time.*
>
> *The professor picked up a box of sand and poured it into the jar. The sand filled the remaining open areas of the jar. "Now," said the professor, "I want you to imagine that this jar signifies your life. The rocks are the truly important things, such as family, health, and relationships. If all else was lost, and only the rocks remained, your life would still be meaningful.*
>
> *"The pebbles are the other things that matter in your life, such as work or school. The sand signifies the remaining 'small stuff*

and material possessions. If you put sand into the jar first, there is no room for the rocks or the pebbles.

"The same can be applied to your lives. If you spend all your time and energy on the small stuff, you will never have room for the truly important things. Pay attention to the things in life that are critical to your happiness and well-being. Take time to get medical checkups, practice self-care, play with your children, go for a run, connect with your spouse, and write your grandmother a letter. There will always be time to go to work, clean the house, or fix the disposal. Take care of the rocks first —things that really matter. Set your priorities. The rest is just pebbles and sand."

Think about the "rocks" in your life. If health is on that list, then self-care should be something you are making time for. We encourage you to take time each week to brainstorm different forms of self-care that make sense for you. Time management and planning ahead are key to a successful implementation!

Self-care also includes seeking out the good things that bring you joy. This idea may sound like a no-brainer, but you'd be amazed at the amount of time we spend going through the motions, ruminating on past events, and focusing on things we want to be different. Finding joy is a conscious choice, not something you have to wait to happen to you. Sophie Cliff, life coach and author of *Choose Joy*, identified some general ideas that research tells us bring about joy. They are connection, prioritizing experiences over things, savoring, movement, practicing kindness, and committing to lifelong learning. We're sure you can relate to these and think of other things that bring you joy.

We know, for some of you, your anxiety may go through the roof if you're not getting something done. This unending quest for completing tasks and fulfilling goals is a learned behavior. This constant messaging of *doing more* comes from a society that tells us checking things off our to-do list equals worthiness and fulfillment. We encourage you to throw your fucking to-do list out the window for a while. If this is panic-inducing, do an item on your list and then take some time out for something that brings you joy. Positive psychology has found many benefits to doing so. It appears that stopping to smell the roses does great things for us. It actually allows us to meet our goals more easily. Taking time out for joy and self-care influences our physical health by boosting our immune system, fighting stress, and decreasing pain. Plus, it feels good, shifts our mood, and gives us a new outlook.

> **Take a deep breath and repeat,**
> ***Shitballs, take care of yourself!***

Dr. Stuart Brown, the founder of the *National Institute for Play*, wrote about our biological need for play. He says play is a necessity, not an afterthought. Work becomes easier when you play because it helps your brain reset. Playing makes our brain function more efficiently. It also provides an opportunity to gain perspective and promotes creative release. Think about some of your goals, such as making more money, getting a promotion, or having a bigger house. There is nothing wrong with having these goals. However, if you're spending so much time on those pursuits that you're not experiencing joy along the way, *that's* where the problem comes in. Otherwise, you may reach your goals only to discover that you're not much happier than you were before. This little story based on Henrich Böll's short story, "The Mexican Fisherman," illustrates this point beautifully. It was first published in 1963 and has since been adapted into many different versions, including the one below.

A boat docked in a tiny Greek village. An American tourist complimented the Greek fisherman on the quality of his fish and asked how long it took him to catch them.

"Not very long," answered the Greek

"But then, why didn't you stay out longer and catch more?" asked the American.

The Greek explained that his small catch was sufficient to meet his needs and those of his family. The American asked, "But what do you do with the rest of your time?"

"I sleep late, fish a little, play with my children, and take a siesta with my wife. In the evenings, I go into the village to see my friends, have a few drinks, play the guitar, and sing a few songs. . . . I have a full life." The American interrupted, "I have an MBA from Harvard and can help you! You should start by fishing longer every day. You can then sell the extra fish you catch. With the extra revenue, you can buy a bigger boat."

"And after that?" asked the Greek.

"With the extra money the larger boat will bring, you can buy a second one and a third one and so on until you have an entire fleet of trawlers. Instead of selling your fish to a middleman, you can then negotiate directly with the processing plants and maybe even open your own plant. You can then leave this little village and move to Athens, Los Angeles, or even New York City! From there, you can direct your huge new enterprise."

"How long would that take?" asked the Greek.

"Twenty, perhaps twenty-five years," replied the American
"And after that?"

"Afterwards? Well, my friend, that's when it gets really interesting," answered the American, laughing. "When your business gets really big, you can start selling stocks and make millions!"

"Millions? Really? And after that?" said the Greek.
"After that, you'll be able to retire, live in a tiny village near the coast, sleep late, play with your children, catch a few fish, take a siesta with your wife, and spend your evenings drinking and enjoying your friends."

Yes, taking stock of what truly makes you happy is essential. So prioritize and then give yourself permission! Marie Kondo, author of *Life-Changing Magic: Spark Joy*, describes this philosophy as *kurashi*, meaning "way of life." We love this idea, so we have to shout out a hell yeah! Even in difficult times, you can still embrace this way of life. You don't have to wait for improved circumstances. We're sure you've experienced this when going through a hard time—*something* brightened your day, whether it was someone who made you laugh, finding comfort snuggling with your dog, talking to a friend, or a moment of peace in nature.

> **Take a deep breath and repeat,**
> *Spark joy!*

Habit-stacking is a fabulous technique that helps you integrate joy and self-care into your daily routine. Take something you already do, like brushing your teeth, driving kids to school, driving to work, washing dishes, or cooking dinner, and link it with a new habit. Stick those suckers right together! So when you brush your teeth, do your calf raises. When you cook, play your favorite music and dance around. When driving the kids, make it fun with sing-alongs you both enjoy. When you're doing dishes, engage in mindful meditation. Habit-stacking makes infusing self-care and joy into your busy day so much easier! We encourage you to give it a try!

✷ It's Your Turn to Play, Explore, and Learn ✷

Self-Care Goal Setting

Set three measurable and meaningful goals related to self-care for this week. Make sure they align with your overall health and well-being goals. For example,

Goal 1: I will set aside time for myself for fifteen minutes a day. I will take this time to journal, deep breathe, and regroup.

Goal 2: I will take ten minutes a day to put on a YouTube exercise video and add movement to my day.

Goal 3: I can habit-stack joy and playfulness by cleaning the house while playing an energizing playlist or listening to an engaging audiobook or podcast. I will plan ahead and create my playlist, borrow an audiobook from the library, or queue up my favorite podcasts before tomorrow.

Social Media/Media Detox Day

There's research floating around out there that the average adult spends approximately eleven hours a day interacting with devices. Why would you possibly want a break from this? It contributes to goddamn stress! It also does not allow you to be present in real-life experiences. Even TV is passive compared to reading a book and using your imagination; they don't call it the idiot box for nothin'. Then there's social media, which is a big fat recipe for comparing yourself and your life to everyone else's. It makes you think, *Damn, everyone's lives are so much more exciting and meaningful than mine.*

Teddy Roosevelt once said, "Comparison is the thief of joy." He would have been down on social media for sure. Social media also instigates the FOMO (fear of missing out) syndrome. When we feel like we're missing experiences everyone else is having, it dampens our own experiences for sure.

Social media detox is a good idea for all these reasons and so many more. If you are glued to your phone for most of the day, it's a sign that you may be addicted! Make a commitment, but be realistic. You don't need to go cold turkey and leave your phone in a drawer for days. Just be conscious of cutting down screen time. If you reach for your phone, take a pause and think, *What else could I do here to engage in life besides looking at this motherfucker?*

✻ Quotes that Support this Mantra and Inspire ✻

- "Self-care is giving the world the best of you, instead of what's left of you."
  —Katie Reed

- "Taking care of yourself doesn't mean me first; it means me too."
  —L.R. Knost

- "I have come to believe that caring for myself is not self-indulgence. It is an act of survival."
  —Audre Lorde

- "With every act of self-care your authentic self gets stronger, and the critical, fearful mind gets weaker. Every act of self-care is a powerful declaration: I am on my side, I am on my side, each day I am more and more on my own side."
  —Susan Weiss Berry

✻ Alternate Mantras for This Topic ✻

- Shitballs, take care of yourself!

- Take care of you (saying it with an accent helps; rewatch *Pretty Woman* for tips).

- I'm worth it (if you remember the commercials or watched *America's Next Top Models*, act it out. Shout out to Maybelline).

- Yo—you fucking matter, so act like it and take care of yourself!

- Spark joy!

✷ Songs to Add to Your Self-Care Playlist ✷

- "Dancing Queen"
    by ABBA

- "Don't Stop Believin'"
    by Journey

- "Don't Stop Me Now"
    by Queen

- "F**kin' Perfect"
    by Pink

- "Good Life"
    by OneRepublic

✷ Further Resources ✷

- *Badass Habits: Cultivate the Awareness, Boundaries, and Daily Upgrades You Need to Make Them Stick*
    by Jen Sincero

- *Burnout: The Secret to Unlocking the Stress Cycle*
    by Emily Nagoski, PhD and Amelia Nagoski, DMA

- *I Am Here Now: A Creative Mindfullness Guide and Journal*
    by The Mindfulness Project

- *Self-Love Workbook for Women: Release Self-Doubt, Build Self-Compassion, and Embrace Who You Are (Self-Love Workbook and Journal)*
    by Megan Logan, MSW

- *Set Boundaries, Find Peace: A Guide to Reclaiming Yourself*
    by Nedra Glover Tawwab

- *The Subtle Art of Not Giving a F*ck: A Counterintuitive Approach to Living a Good Life*
    by Mark Mason (now a movie!)

- *The Life-Changing Magic of Tidying Up: The Japanese Art of Decluttering and Organizing*
    by Marie Kondo

- Play: How It Shapes our Brain, Opens the Imagination, and Invigorates the Soul!
    by Stuart Brown, MD, and Christopher Vaughan

"If your compassion does not include yourself,
it is incomplete."

—Jack Kornfield

Respect and consideration for ourselves seems like a no-brainer, right? While it may seem obvious, it's incredible how many of us value other people's feelings, thoughts, and needs more than our own. Sometimes, we even go as far as absorbing other people's pain or bad moods like a sponge. When we take on these negative feelings, we are not allowing ourselves to be a separate entity and only feel comfortable when everyone around us is happy. Does that sound exhausting? It is! It's also a key ingredient in burnout. If you're a person who puts the needs of others first or has been called a "people pleaser," you've most likely experienced that moment when you hit a wall. You know, that moment when you think, *To hell with everybody else. I'm taking care of myself for a while!*

This mantra invites awareness and practice in the art of balancing our own needs with those around us. It's along the same lines as learning to be assertive, as opposed to being passive or aggressive. Eastern philosophies incorporate self-compassion more readily than our "pull yourself up by the bootstraps" Western world. The Dalai Lama comments about self-love in Daniel Goleman's book *Destructive Emotions: Accounts of Conversations with the Dalai Lama*:

> *Now he* (the Dalai Lama) *made a long point in Tibetan about how in his view, caring for oneself and others is fundamental to human existence, and that to leave out the self in the Western view of compassion is a drastic omission. In essence, compassion is more than a simple feeling for another—empathy—but a concerned, heartfelt caring, wanting to do something to relieve the person's suffering. And that holds whether the being involved is the self, someone else, or an animal.*

When was the last time you gave yourself *heartfelt* caring? And we mean the whole you, flaws and all! Buddhist practice encourages us to be as kind and forgiving to ourselves as we are to others. Their teachings say that you deserve love and affection as much as anyone in the universe. Buddhism points out that it is very difficult to be kind and caring toward others if we are not taking care of and being kind to ourselves. Think about that for a moment. To give others our all, we need to give ourselves that same level of love and care. This is certainly a worthy endeavor that we can all improve upon. We're not saying you should be narcissistic or self-absorbed. There's a difference between *exclusively* honoring yourself and balancing this with respecting others. In another Eastern traditional practice, Hinduism, they have a beautiful greeting that implies a balance between honoring yourself and others: namaste. Some say it is two people making a pact to celebrate the best parts of each other and letting the rest fall away. The greeting has many interpretations, but they all imply the following:

> *"I honor the place in you*

Where the entire universe resides
I honor the place in you
Of love, of light, of peace
I honor the place in you
Where if you are in that place in you and I am in that place in me
There is only one of us."

What a great way to say hello to someone, right?

> **Remember and repeat,**
> ***Kindness must include myself, or something is missing!***

If, after reading the last few pages, you start to wonder what the difference is between self-compassion and self-esteem, you are not alone. They both significantly impact our mental health. Here's where they differ: self-esteem is dependent on our evaluation of our worthiness as well as other people's opinions of us. Self-compassion is not. For example, when you kick ass on a project at work, your self-esteem goes up, and then it goes in the crapper if you feel like you blurted out inappropriate comments. It's like a pendulum, going back and forth. As Dr. Kristin Neff, a pioneer in the field of self-compassion, so eloquently explained, "The positive emotions of self-compassion kick in exactly when self-esteem falls down; when we don't meet our expectations or fail in some way." Self-compassion is constant. All day, all the time. Once you start practicing it, you may realize you've been your own worst enemy! Criticizing yourself turns on that fight, flight, or freeze stress response, which increases your cortisol because you don't feel safe. Self-compassion does the opposite. It's soothing. It's like when you were a kid and scraped your knee, and after your mom comforted you, you could go back to playing. *Be your own mom!* You'll feel safe, cared for, and loved instead of feeling criticized and isolated, which leads to rumination and anxiety. You just have to learn to interrupt your own dickish comments to yourself. It all goes back to mindfulness, guys!

Being human means having the full Monty of feelings, moods, and thoughts, including the good, the bad, and the ugly. We just aren't meant to have *only* good times, pleasant dispositions, and positive thoughts. There are very practical reasons for the negative stuff. In the old days, as cavemen, our survival depended on this type of anxious, worried thinking that kept us hyperalert for any danger or disharmony in our clans or groups. It's your built-in defense mechanism. Embracing that being human includes negativity will make you more prepared and equipped to productively handle tough situations and feelings. Dan Millman, the amazing American author, talks about the power of accepting the dark aspects in yourself, which he calls the shadow, in his book, *Everyday Enlightenment*. Check out this modified quote from his book:

> For some of us, personal growth has become a never-ending self-improvement program —working to develop a nicer, happier, more secure personality. Even talented, wealthy, successful people remain restless, anxious, and insecure if they hide behind a social mask. We find self-esteem through authenticity and self-compassion, which comes when we see both our light and our shadow. Embracing the shadow is one of the most powerful shifts a human being can make.

He goes on to clarify the shadow: "Illuminating your shadow is not about inviting the devil to dinner or allowing negative qualities or impulses to influence your behavior. When you have seen your dark side, you can make a clearer choice about how you will behave."

So, as you learn to have compassion for yourself and embrace all the beautiful, wonderful, weird, and downright crazy aspects of who you are, you can begin the process of consciously choosing to act on behalf of your positive self. But never forget or deny that you have a shadow. And when it shows itself, you know what to do: shine the light of compassion on it without judgment and then choose to act on behalf of your light.

We love the following Native American parable emphasizing that we *all* have these destructive emotions. Once we're aware of them, we can choose which emotions to focus on.

> **Remember and repeat,**
> *We all have light and dark; embrace the light!*

A Native American wisdom story tells of an old Cherokee who is teaching his grandson about life. "A fight is going on inside me," he said to the boy. "It is a terrible fight, and it is between two wolves. One is evil—he is anger, envy, sorrow, regret, greed, arrogance, self-pity, guilt, resentment, inferiority, lies, false pride, superiority, and ego. The other is good—he is joy, peace, love, hope, serenity, humility, kindness, benevolence, empathy, generosity, truth, compassion, and faith. The same fight is going on inside you—and inside every other person, too." The grandson thought about it for a minute and then asked his grandfather, "Which wolf will win?" The old Cherokee simply replied, "The one you feed."

A ton of people look to the external world these days to find acceptance because it is easier than the alternative: looking inside ourselves. The problem is we can get bigger and better things, obtain prestige and fame, master difficult skills, and reach goal after goal and still feel empty. Not that it's bad to do these things; it just won't give us that feeling we wanted in the first place. You know, the sense of being enough the way we are. Our quest to be "enough" is driven by our basic needs for love and security. These innate needs are often neglected instead of nurtured because taking care of our emotional selves is not often emphasized in our culture. So go forth and work on accepting and honoring the person you are, *and we mean the whole damn you!* Embrace your uniqueness, brilliantness, your little idiosyncrasies, and the not-so-flattering qualities that make up the person that you are. The positive psychologist Robert Holden said, "No amount of self-improvement can make up for a lack of self-acceptance." We couldn't agree more! Now is the time to start being kind and loving to the one person in the world who will remain your constant companion. You will find it much easier to choose positive actions and feel love toward others once you have acknowledged all the sides of yourself. Remember to keep in mind that other people also have these different and unique sides to them. When you accept and embrace yourself, doing the same for others will naturally follow. You will be more aware of the humanness that connects us all and be more willing to empathize with others as you wrap the warm and fuzzy blanket of compassion around your own self.

✻ It's Your Turn to Play, Explore, and Learn ✻

The Inner Critic

My Salty Inner Critic

We'll be tapping into our visualization skills and imagination for this exercise. Start by creating an image separate from yourself that will represent your inner critic. Come up with as many details as you can. Do they have a silly voice like Donald Duck, Bugs Bunny, or a pirate? How about glasses that are down on their nose? A baseball cap? Are they a llama, garden gnome, or an actor? Take a few minutes until you have a good image. If you enjoy drawing, we encourage you to sketch your inner critic in your journal. Having a visual representation reminds us that the inner critic is no joke and, for some, loud and bossy as hell.

It is essential for us to realize that this inner critic is not *who we are*. Consider it as the judgy, know-it-all part of your brain who *loves* to criticize you! And bless their hearts, our nitpicking inner critic works tirelessly to keep us safe from the slightest possibility of being hurt, failing, or getting rejected. Unfortunately, the IC's eagerness (going cool acronym-dropping on you now) keeps us from growth, change, and opportunities. The IC *must* be kept in check. It is imperative to our well-being! Learn to recognize its disparaging arrival so you can give your fault-finding jerk of an IC the bird and silence it with facts or a kickass mantra. This may sound extreme, but trust us, firmness is necessary!

The Wise Counselor

The wise counselor is the opposite of the inner critic. Create a persona of a wise, helpful, compassionate, all-knowing little Buddha buddy. This can be your dog (dogs are so wise), your cat, your mom, a treasured friend, a deer, Oprah, Chuck Norris, Yoda, Shrek, The Dude from *The Big Lebowski* . . . the sky's the limit! Pick whoever you feel is a comforting presence. Again, have fun and sketch a representation. Work with your wise counselor and craft helpful, balanced, healthy thoughts. Your wise counselor is always inside you, full of compassion and love.

✳ Inspirational Quotes to Support This Mantra ✳

- "You have been criticizing yourself for years, and it hasn't worked. Try approving of yourself and see what happens."
  —Louise Hay

- "Self-compassion is simply giving the same kindness to ourselves that we would give to others."
  —Christopher Germer

- "Talk to yourself like you would talk to someone you love."
  —Brené Brown

- "When you find peace within yourself, you become the kind of person who can live at peace with others."
  —Peace Pilgrim

✶ Alternate Mantra Ideas for This Topic ✶

- I accept the best and worst of myself.

- I honor myself and those around me.

- I am worthy of compassion.

- We all have light and dark; embrace the light.

✶ Songs to Add to Your Self-Compassion Playlist ✶

- "Beautiful"
  by Christina Aguilera

- "Good as Hell"
  by Lizzo

- "I Wanna Get Better"
  by Bleachers

- "Scars to Your Beautiful"
  by Alessia Cara

- "True Colors"
  by Cindi Lauper

✶ Further Resources ✶

- *The Mindful Self-Compassion Workbook: A Proven Way to Accept Yourself, Build Inner Strength, and Thrive* by Christopher Germer and Kristen Neff

- *A Way of Being*
    by Carl Rogers

- *I am F*cking Radiant: A Self-Care Journal to Help You Ditch the Spa Days, Quit the Bullsh*t, and Actually Feel F*cking Better (Calendars & Gifts to Swear By)*
    by Annie Sarac

- *Everyday Enlightenment: The Twelve Gateways to Personal Growth*
    by Dan Millman

- *The Highly Sensitive Person*
    by Elaine Aron

Just Breathe, Damn It

Sticky Note Mantras

> "Feelings come and go like clouds in a windy sky.
> Conscious breathing is my anchor."
> —Thich Nhat Hang

OBVIOUSLY, WE MUST breathe to live, but breathing can be much more than an involuntary physical function. It's also an extremely powerful biological mechanism that most of us typically ignore. If you tend to take shallow breaths and then have a stressful event like losing your car keys when you needed to be out the door ten minutes ago, you may be in for the joy of a panic attack! In this situation, paying attention to your breath can calm, comfort, and empower you. Check out the science outlining the benefits, and we guarantee you'll jump on the conscious breathing bandwagon.

Breathing is so elemental that we often discount its impact, thinking, *How can something I already do every second of every day be helpful?* The crucial difference lies in learning to do it *consciously and effectively*. Sometimes, simple things can make a huge difference. Remember the KISS principle from the introduction? Here it is again:

K—Keep I—It S—Simple S—Stupid. Breathing hits the KISS principle bullseye! It's so easy, portable, cheap, and effective.

Conveniently located and handy, your breath is always with you, ready to be a tool to calm and comfort you. Deep, controlled breathing initiates a  physiological and biochemical reaction called the relaxation response (mentioned in previous chapters). A deep sigh of relief is an example of controlled breathing. After one big, slow breath out, the tension and anxiety will begin to exit the stage. Now your body and brain start to say, "All right, all right, everyone calm down, nothing to see here. Let's move along." The scientific community is moving away from medicinal fixes and returning to more natural and traditional remedies. In other words, we are shifting from a "let me write you a prescription" to more of a "try something natural first." We have heard this described as simply *skills not pills*. For example, traditional Western medical practitioners are now routinely recommending exercise and a healthy diet to eliminate the need for certain medications. The same thing goes for mindfulness and controlled breathing as an intervention for anxiety, stress, gloomy moods, chronic pain, focus or sleep issues, and poor digestion.

> **Take a deep, slow breath and ask yourself,**
> *Is my breath happening to me, or am I doing my breathing?*

Today, we can measure the physical effects of deep breathing on the mind and body. With instruments like biofeedback, we can actually see how strategies like controlled breathing can initiate positive physiological and biochemical changes in the body. Studies show it does all sorts of great things, like lowering your heart rate, blood pressure, and stress-related hormones. It also releases our feel-good neurochemical friends, serotonin and dopamine.

Scientists have collected mounds of data showing that stress hormones are related to poor mental and physical health. Prolonged heightened cortisol levels are linked with terrible side effects, such as impaired cognitive function, suppressed thyroid function, blood sugar imbalance, higher blood pressure, lowered immunity, and our all-time favorite . . . increased abdominal fat. *Booooooooo*! The reason this last issue is so important is not because we may bust our pant buttons but because this increase in fat is associated with higher LDL cholesterol, heart attacks, and even strokes. You can't always avoid stressful activities, but you can take charge and manage your body's reaction through your breath. The best part about this is there are no prescriptions needed!

> **Close your eyes and repeat,**
> *Just breathe . . . (damn it!).*

Let's review some physiological basics. You have an autonomic nervous system with two parts: the sympathetic (fight-or-flight response) and the parasympathetic (relaxation response). Stress, strong emotions, or thinking about things that have caused stress or strong emotions triggers the fight-or-flight response. This stress is interpreted by the part of your brain called the amygdala, which doesn't do things subtly. *Go big, or go home* is its motto. When it interprets stress or danger, it quickly fires up the sympathetic nervous system, and that's when all kinds of shit hits the fan. The issue at hand is that the

PARAsympathetic: think PARAchute..... it's your escape route from stress.

amygdala is so concerned with protecting us that it sets off alarms and physical responses even when it isn't warranted. Like when your boss drops by your cubicle at work to tell you that he gave you the wrong information, so you'll have to redo your current project. He graciously adds that you don't need to worry; you won't have to present to the company for another hour or two. Well . . . shit! The sympathetic nervous system is set into action. Fight-or-flight is in full effect! Your body and brain are being flooded with adrenaline and other icky stress-inducing hormones. Your heart beats faster, and your breathing speeds up and becomes shallow. News flash—short, rapid breathing is not going to help you out here. In this emotionally stressful situation, you need to be aware of your breathing and make a conscious effort to set off your *para*sympathetic nervous system.

This mantra was inspired by Drew Barrymore's character in *Ever After*. Drew, who is playing the role of Cinderella, is getting ready to make her grand entrance into the ball to meet her dream guy. You know the story, right? She's freaking out because she's not supposed to be at the ball but braves the wrath of her evil stepmother to see the dashing prince. As she looks out over the party and all the guests, she says to herself, *Breathe. Just breathe.* If you haven't seen this movie and need a little imaginative help, imagine a person walking into a vast sports arena ready to compete or to a podium in front of a large audience about to give a speech. Visualize them standing offstage or in the entrance tunnel. See them close their eyes and take a deep breath. This deep, slow breath does wonders to calm the nerves, kick in the courage, and helps them to take a big step forward.

One of our alternate mantras, *breathe through it*, speaks to how conscious breathing helps us remain calm and push forward, even when we don't necessarily want to. Yes, a deep, slow breath helps get our shit together so our mind and body can function optimally. Controlled breath is known as a *bottom-up approach,* meaning that we are working through the body to help the mind. So, next time you're freaking out, you know what to do. Just. Breathe. Damn it.

✲ It's Your Turn to Play, Explore, and Learn ✲

One-Minute Breathing Check-In

In this exercise, you will be timing yourself for one minute and counting the number of inhales and exhales you take. No peeking ahead! Do the counting first, then find out what your breathing says about you.

- When you are ready, set a one-minute timer, close your eyes, and begin.

- If you took more than twenty breaths in that minute, you are likely feeling quite anxious.

- Take a few minutes and practice a few slow, deep breaths, with the exhalation longer than the inhalation.

- Now, try the minute timer again. Your goal is to decrease your number of breaths to four or five breaths per minute. This activates your parasympathetic nervous system and relaxation response.

4-4-4-4 Breathing or Box Breathing

Navy seals, real-life badasses who know a thing or two about stressful situations, use this technique.

- Inhale through the nose for four seconds.

- Hold for four seconds.

- Exhale through your mouth for four seconds.

- Hold for four seconds and repeat the cycle.

Diaphragm Breathing (DB)

DB is marvelous because it engages your most effective and efficient muscle designed for breathing, your diaphragm. It's not just for singing!

Try it before bed if you have trouble sleeping or anytime you want to calm your system. Your thoughts most likely will be wandering, and that's okay. Just turn the focus back to your breath.

> *Start with your hands resting on your belly, just below your belly button.*
>
> *Think about trying to blow up a balloon in your stomach.*
>
> *Exhale slowly, with pursed lips like you are blowing on a hot bowl of soup. This will help you get a longer exhale. Let everything go.*
>
> *Move the hand on your ribs to your upper chest, just below the collarbone. As you inhale, breathe into your belly, allowing your ribs to expand and your upper chest to broaden.*
>
> *As you exhale, think of a balloon losing air slowly and deflating. Let everything go.*
>
> *Repeat this sequence three to four times.*
>
> <u>*A visualization to add to this:*</u>
>
> *Close your eyes and imagine your breath is taking you to a safe place.*
>
> *It takes you to a place with peace, tranquility, and calmness.*
>
> *As you think about this place, let the breath calm, comfort, and relax you.*

The Buzzing Bee Breath for Relaxation

The Buzzing Bee Breath is a common exercise found in yoga classes. When done correctly, it triggers your vagus nerve, creating a feeling of peace and serenity. Research shows it helps to reduce heart rate, induce relaxation, and make you feel less cranky or downright irritable.

- Find a spot to sit comfortably on the floor or your favorite chair.

- Close your eyes and focus on relaxing the muscles in your face. Start from the forehead down to your chin and neck. Scan your body for pain or tightness and slowly let go of any tension you are holding.

- Now put your index fingers and thumbs on the little bump of skin and cartlidge connecting your face and ear hole. If you are looking for a more technical term, it's called your tragus cartilage (TC). Inhale and gently apply pressure to your TC with your fingers.

- Slowly exhale your breath through your teeth, making a loud buzzing or humming sound. This is a form of chanting, which calms the nervous system. And it prompts a longer exhale as well.

❋ Inspirational Quotes that Support This Mantra ❋

- "Inhale the future. Exhale the past."
  —Unknown

- "Are you a stingy breather? Well, don't be. Be extravagant with your breathing and come fully alive."
  —Ron Fletcher

- "Take a deep breath. It calms the mind."
  —Regina Brett

- "You can take from every experience what it has to offer you. And you cannot be defeated if you just keep taking one breath followed by another."
  —Oprah Winfrey

- "You don't always need a plan. Sometimes, you just need to breathe, trust, let go and see what happens."
  —Mandy Hale

✳ Alternate Mantras for This Topic ✳

- Breathe through it.

- Inhale the good shit; exhale the bullshit.

- My breath comforts me.

- Inhale, exhale. That's how I'll get through it.

- Let your breath guide you.

✳ Songs to Add to Your Breathe Playlist ✳

- "Breathe (2 AM)"
  by Anna Nalick

- "Breathe"
  by Taylor Swift

- "Breathe in Breathe Out"
  by Mat Kearny

- "Still Breathing"
  by Green Day

- "The Breath You Take"
  by George Strait

✳ Further Resources ✳

- *Breathing: The Master Key to Self-Healing*
  by Andrew Weil, MD (Audio)

- *Science of Breath: A Practical Guide*
  by Swami Rama, Rudolph Ballentine, and Alan Hymes

- *The Cortisol Connection: Why Stress Makes You Fat and Ruins Your Health and What You Can Do About It*
  by Shawn Talbott and William Kraemer (Foreword)

- *The Stress Effect*
  by Richard Weinstein

Talk to Your Soul

Sticky Note Mantras

> "A moment in silence, a talk with your soul . . .
> is a moment of self-reflection,
> a nourishment for life, to create a whole new world."
> —Unknown

SELF-REFLECTION. INTROSPECTION. It's hard to make time for it, right? You've probably heard it's beneficial but are unsure how or where to begin. Or, like most of us, you're way too busy to slow down and do something like this. Think of it this way: taking the time to reflect is a good investment. It helps us accept our current stressors, circumstances, and emotions. It also reduces negative or uncomfortable feelings. Just like when you pour your heart out to your therapist or friend, you feel a little better, no? Once you get your thoughts out and mull them over, it's like Harry Potter jumps out and says "Reducto!" to those crappy feelings, and a weight is lifted off your shoulders. Journaling is a simple way to do this daily; no friend or therapist is needed. And there are bound to be times when you can't find anyone to vent to. As an anonymous journal enthusiast once said, "Sometimes only the paper will listen to you." Studies have shown many physical, cognitive, and emotional benefits of journaling. It reduces anxiety, improves the awareness and perception of events, stops obsessive thinking, regulates emotions, and boosts physical health. It's easy to do, takes no cash out of your pocket, and can be rather fun if you doodle and throw in some cuss words. It's also helpful to recognize those automatic thoughts your brain keeps sneaking in, encouraging you to live with more purpose and intention. So, basically, it won't hurt you, and more than likely, you will get something out of it.

Journaling helps create detachment or cognitive defusion, which means taking a step back from your thoughts instead of being hyperfocused on them. This separation encourages you to take your thoughts for what they are—just thoughts, not facts. Writing them down gets you to notice them and move through them instead of trying to eliminate, ruminate, or act on them. This goes for feelings too. Don't try to hold onto them; just *notice them*. The Dalai Lama has great remarks about letting go of feelings: "We confuse happiness with the elimination of negative feelings when it is the ability to receive the pleasant without grasping and the unpleasant without condemning." In other words, let them flow and be aware of them, but don't try to stop them or hold onto them. All feelings serve their purpose. Anxiety and fear protect us from threats, anger tells us something is wrong, and even guilt can lead to growth, prompting us to make amends if needed. Emotions are fluid. The sooner we accept this, the more satisfaction we will have.

There are no hard-and-fast rules about journaling, but here are some tips to help you get started:

- Begin with a small amount of time each day. Creating a regular time is helpful, but flexibility is key since shit always comes up.

- Decide what medium you enjoy. Do you prefer an app on your phone, a notebook, or a guided journal with prompts? Maybe writing on the computer is better for you? You may be writing about heavy stuff, which can get uncomfortable. However, journaling doesn't always have to be serious or productive. Think of it as a creative outlet and a stress reliever rather than just an intellectual activity.

- Check out the exercises at the end of this chapter for plenty of thought-provoking questions. A blank page staring at you can be intimidating, so integrate some prompts until you get a rhythm going.

Teasing out your automatic thoughts is always beneficial and something to include in your journal on a regular basis. There's a process called the ABC model that is incredibly helpful. Think about situations that you get stuck on, cause you distress, or make you uncomfortable. There's usually a limiting belief lurking around! Plug in the events, thoughts, and feelings into the following model.

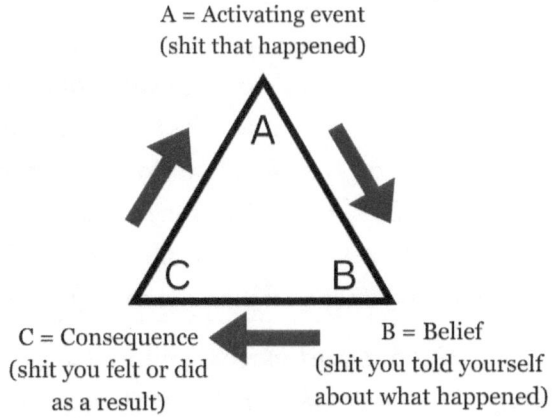

This process is like being your own therapist but cheaper and less time-consuming. You'd be surprised how often the thoughts you've been telling yourself are unrealistic, unnecessary rubbish. Once you're aware of the bullshit, you can move on to the process of figuring out what would be a helpful thought. It's a perfect time for a mantra . . . hell yeah!

✴ Helene ✴

HERE'S AN EXAMPLE from my life to give you an idea of the ABC model:

A. A: I didn't get much writing accomplished today.

B. B: My writing is not good enough. It's incoherent, and my sentence structure has gone out the window. I don't know why I'm doing this project; no one will read it.

C. C: I feel like a loser.

Here's me working through the process of evaluation and redirection:

Yes, I didn't get as much editing done as I would have liked today. That doesn't mean the whole project is a wash. Not *all of it* is incoherent. I'm telling myself the project has to be perfect to be valuable. This goes along with a core belief that I'm not good enough. I notice I think that way a lot. I want to do things perfectly or not do them at all. This stupid, self-defeating expectation shuts me down with fear and makes it harder to enjoy the process of writing and life, for that matter. I looked up some quotes on perfection and found Margaret Atwood's quote, "If I waited for perfection, I would never write a word." Yes! My new thought is, ***Of course***, *it's not perfect! I wrote it!* I feel so much better after working through that.

> **Get out your journal and write,**
> ***Talking to my soul makes me live more intentionally!***

~

Another theme to bring up and identify in your journal is the stuff that's in and out of your control. Of course, we want to spend our energy on things we can do something about. So, make this topic a regular entry in your journal, guys. Practice makes permanent (that's mantra material right there!). Draw a good-sized circle. Make sure it is big enough to write in. Now write the things you can control inside of the circle. Outside the circle, jot down things that are out of your control. Beth has provided an example about trying to eat healthier, something we can all relate to! The process of writing it down lets you zero in on what you can control. Wrapping up, you've got nothing to lose by trying journaling. If it's really not your thing, find another way to reflect such as art. Artistic expressions can be anything that speaks to your artistic heart, such as poems, narratives, and artwork are introspective and a great alternative. Just going for a walk can put you in touch with your soul if you ask yourself tough questions. As you move your body, you are also moving through these thoughts and feelings. It's an easy and natural form of bilateral stimulation, which is a rhythmic pattern of left-right stimuli, similar to the technique used in EMDR therapy. It will be difficult sometimes, but keep on trucking, and stick with the process of reflection. On average, it takes around *sixty-six days for a new behavior to become automatic.* So, stick with it for two months, and you're golden!

Problem: I need to lose some weight so I feel better.

Food choices, meal prep, voicing my needs to my family, prioritizing healthy eating, shopping for easy meals, getting some movement in every day, eating mindfully and slowly, staying away from the break room at work, bringing my own snacks with me.

My kids bringing junk food into the house, my husband's schedule, tempting food in the break room, the cost of healthy food, injuries, orthopedic challenges, my work hours, the weather, distance to the gym

Beth looking at the junk food in the pantry

✳ It's Your Turn to Play, Explore, and Learn ✳

<u>Journal Prompts</u>

- What are your go-to coping strategies when stressed out?

- How do you deal with change at work, home, and in relationships?

- Ask yourself the magic wand question: Imagine all your problems are solved while sleeping. When you wake up, what's different? Think about specifics here.

- What's your most important intention for today? What is your plan to complete it?

- Create an affirmation to focus on this week.

- What pumps you up and gives you energy? Conversely, what drains the crap out of you?

- What were some of your favorite moments today? Feel free to draw or doodle them!

- Who or what makes you feel safe, valued, and loved?

- Write a letter to your future self and tell them how you're doing now.

✸ Inspirational Quotes that Support This Mantra ✸

- "In the journal I am at ease."
  —Anaïs Nin

- "All the noise in my brain. I clamp it to the page so it will be still."
  —Barbara Kingsolver

- "Journal writing is a voyage to the interior."
  —Christina Baldwin

- "The unexamined life is not worth living."
  —Socrates

- "I shall live badly if I do not write, and I shall write badly if I do not live."
  —Françoise Sagan

✸ Alternate Mantras for This Topic ✸

- Reflect and move forward.

- Examine, check, and change.

- My journey starts with journaling.

- Self-discovery is my greatest challenge.

✶ Songs to Add to Your Reflection Playlist ✶

- "In the Meantime"
    by Dolly Parton

- "Some of It"
    by Eric Church

- "Gilrs Like Us"
    by Zoe Wess

- "Thank You"
    by Dido

- "7 Years"
    by Lukas Graham

✶ Further Resources ✶

- *Knock Knock, I'm so Freaking Freaked Out Inner Truth Journal*
    by Knock Knock

- *True You: A Self-Discovery Journal of Prompts and Exercises to Inspire Reflection and Growth*
    by Dr. Kelly Vincent (author) and Vicentra Key (illustrator)

- *The Great Book of Journaling: How Journal Writing Can Support a Life of Wellness, Creativity, Meaning and Purpose (How to Journaling Self-Help)*
    by Eric Maisel PhD and Lynda Monk MSW RSW CPCC

- *Soul Therapy: A 365 Day Journal for Self Exploration, Healing and Reflection*
    by Positive Soul and Jacqueline Kademian

- *Wreck This Journal*
    by Keri Smith

- *Self-Love Workbook for Women: Release Self-Doubt, Build Self-Compassion, and Embrace Who You Are*
    by Megan Logan

The Mind and Body: BFF's

Sticky Note Mantras

> "The mind and body are not separate units, but one integrated system. How we act and what we think, eat, and feel are all related to our health."
> —Bernie Siegel, M.D.

THERE'S NO DENYING the inseparable link between our thoughts, emotions, and physical sensations. If the mind and body were teenagers, they'd be passing little folded-up notes to each other all day in class. Yeah, it's probably all texting now, but you get the idea. They communicate constantly, and what one does impacts the other. For example, toxic thoughts not only bring us into a negative headspace, but they also cause our body to release all those icky chemicals and hormones, which leads to things like increased heart rate, stomach problems, headaches, and muscle tension. Positive thinking, on the other hand, boosts our disposition and physical health. Healthy eating influences not only the body but also our mindset, and this extends to conditions beyond your immediate mood. In 2023, Tori DeAngelis wrote about this in an article for the American Psychological Association.

> We know that what we eat affects our physical health—that a diet loaded with french fries and burgers is worse for our hearts and waistlines than one that includes regular helpings of steamed broccoli and brown rice.
>
> Less well-known are how food can influence our mental health—not just our immediate mood but also symptoms of depression, anxiety, attention-deficit/hyperactivity disorder (ADHD), and other conditions.

She goes on to discuss a new movement called nutritional psychology, which explores the relationship between food and mental health. Basically, she says it can no longer be ignored, motherfuckers! Yes, integrated mind-body health approaches have moved to the forefront. Nutrition, exercise, positive thinking, mindfulness, deep breathing, gratitude—all of this impacts your mental and physical health at the same time. Heightening our awareness involving these connections puts us on the path to better well-being.

One of the biggest influences on your mental health in your body is your gut. People say, "go with your gut" for a reason. It is your second brain, with over one hundred million neurons in the walls of your intestinal nervous system. That's more than your spinal cord! Deepak Chopra, kick-ass alternative medicine advocate, comments on this: "As mental health is increasingly connected to the body, it's becoming clear that a faraway region like the intestine, and its population of micro-organisms known as the microbiome, plays a major role in a person's moods and general susceptibility to anxiety and depression."

So, your gut affects your mood, and vice versa. A long nerve from your gut to your brain called the vagus nerve makes it possible for information to be conveyed in milliseconds. The communication is a little one-sided here. Ninety percent of the neurons in the vagus nerve carry information from the gut to the brain, not vice versa. This means the signals generated in the gut massively affect the brain. A whopping 95 percent of serotonin, the feel-good chemical boosting mood and emotions, is produced in the gastrointestinal tract. So, your gut doesn't just digest food, it impacts how you feel. People with nourishing, varied gut microbes have better moods and overall mental health. If you frequent fast-food joints and prefer processed foods (you know who you are!), we want you to know that it's not too late to start building up good bacteria. Only 10 percent of adults meet the recommendation of the USDA dietary guidelines, so you're not alone! If you want to evaluate your intestinal health, type in "gut intelligence test" on Google, and it will give you access to more than you ever wanted to know about your gut!

We want to shoot for eating nutrient-dense food. You know, stuff that gives us a lot of vitamins and minerals and not a lot of sugar, sodium, and saturated fat. Unfortunately, the grocery store can be the ultimate shitshow. Prepacked foods line the aisles with many preservatives staring at you, saying, "Buy *me*! I'm cheap, yummy, *and* easy to heat up in the microwave." This is where you make a harsh U-turn with your cart and scramble out of the frozen foods section! It's a good rule of thumb to go for items that grow naturally and don't come in a package.

Watch out for sugar—it's like a scheming drug dealer planning to get you hooked in aisle seven. In 2013, Professor Schroeder of Connecticut College and his students conducted an infamous research experiment. Lab rats were repeatedly put in a labyrinth where they had a choice between getting a hit of cocaine or getting a lab rat-sized Oreo cookie treat. Which do you think the lab rats chose? We'll give you a hint: it wasn't cocaine! This means that these highly processed, sugar-laden, saturated fatty foods are not only irresistible, tasty little morsels, but they are also addictive as fuck! So unless you live on a deserted island without access to processed foods, your brain knows this shit is good. Like . . . *real* good.

Companies spend millions on taste science research. These taste scientists' main goal is to engineer food that is very hard to stop eating. The brain remembers that delectable feeling of being satiated by hydrogenated oils and corn syrup-filled goodness and the hit of dopamine and energy it provided. All this adds up to the *joy of cravings*! Cravings are pretty badass at hijacking our thoughts and sense of reasoning; that shit goes right out the window when a treat is presented to us, and that's when we skip down the path of indulgence. The same parts of the brain that are involved in addiction are involved in cravings, and they're damn good at their jobs! So, for people who struggle with addiction, impulsive eating, or tilt toward the habits of excess, sugar can be a huge dilemma. Sugar is not only really bad for you, but it also contributes to emotional eating because it gives us a dopamine hit or a bit of a lift. It is hard to resist a dose of feel-good chemicals.

The former FDA commissioner, Dr. David Kessler, stresses that overeating is a habitual response. Evolutionary-wise, food was more scarce, and having some padding was a good idea and posed less of a threat to our survival. In more recent times, many of us have developed the habit of eating during emotionally stressful times for comfort. Every time you feel stressed or upset, these feelings cue your body to eat. The power of habit strikes again! Just like our habits of thought, we must first recognize that these habits are no longer useful. Then, dial up your awareness and insert a pause before you eat. If you are not hungry but reacting to a feeling, *refuse the cue to overeat.* If you pause and refuse the cue many times, you will develop a new habit. This takes a lot of awareness! Dr. Kessler advocates for visualizing and playing the tape to the end in your mind of what will happen if you go with the old habit. Usually, it's something like, *I'll feel good for two minutes, and then I'll feel horrible.* Eventually, *not* doing the old habit will slowly become what you feel good about.

We put together some protective factors for you to consider regarding nutrition and mental health.

- **Eat regularly.** The idea here is to keep your blood sugar levels constant. If they drop, you're susceptible to the hangry syndrome of feeling tired and grumpy. It's a biochemical reaction due to low blood sugar plus the release of adrenaline and cortisol. The good news is that there is an easy cure: stuff your cakehole! Prevention is easy. Plan ahead and pack some healthy snacks.

- **Eat mindfully.** Notice how your food looks, tastes, smells, and feels in your body as you eat it. Savor your food and chew slowly.

- **Drink up!** Dehydration seriously screws up your mood, energy, and concentration levels. Carry a water bottle with you when you're on the go!

- **Eat lots of good fats.** We're talking about olive oil, seeds, fish, avocados, milk, and eggs here. These support your brain! Stay away from trans fats found in packaged foods. These can bring your mood down and negatively impact your heart too.

- **Fruits and veggies.** These give you the vitamins and minerals your brain and body need to stay healthy physically and mentally. And eating them makes you feel good! Shoot for a few cups of each a day.

- **Don't forget the protein.** Protein contains amino acids that regulate your mood. Get a little in at each meal.

We encourage you to take a few moments and think about areas you want to improve. We're sure everyone can put *eat more fruits and veggies* on the list! List three small things you want to do differently each day and track it for a week. This encourages accountability, which we all need. Even if you don't check off all three changes daily, it will still make a positive difference. If you're trying to lose weight, research shows that by making three one hundred calorie changes each day, you'll be thirty pounds lighter by the end of a year. Above all, recognize the strong connection between your mental and physical health. Eat mindfully and intentionally. Dr. Will Cole, author of *The Inflammation Spectrum*, says,

I wish people knew that mental health is not separate from physical health. Mental health is physical health. I wish they knew that inflammation was the underlying trigger of issues like anxiety, depression, brain fog, and fatigue. I wish they knew that hormones, gut health, nutrient deficiencies, environmental toxins, chronic stress, and unresolved trauma are all factors that drive inflammation. But most of all, I wish they knew they weren't inherently broken and that healing was so profoundly possible.

Preach on, dude!

> **Remember and repeat,**
> *The mind and body strongly affect each other!*

Let's talk about movement. Exercise is like a magic elixir that nurtures your mental health. Your mind and body are fully connected; when one is not cared for, the other will suffer. Movement staves off things like headaches, stomach aches, muscle aches, inflammation, immune issues . . . the list goes on. It leads to better sleep, enhanced mood, and increased focus and energy. It also releases the feel-good endorphins—dopamine, norepinephrine, and serotonin. Moving your body also quiets some of that constant chatter in your brain. It gets you in the moment, alleviating stress, anxiety, and rumination. Just like eating good stuff, exercise makes changes in your brain. *Who knew you had this much power?* It's like taking medication without the side effects and cost. Not to mention all the stuff it does for your physical health. Exercise influences your cardiovascular health and blood pressure. And ooh la la la, it also enhances your sex life too! It takes about thirty minutes a day for three to five days a week to see huge benefits, but if you're not there yet, just do what you can and build up to it. Here are some tips to get you started:

- **Find some form of exercise you enjoy.** Finding the right fit for you is not rocket science, but it's important to consider if you want to make it a lasting habit. We encourage you to mix it up! You want to keep it novel and fun so it doesn't become boring, and your sneakers end up in the back of your closet.

- **Think of it as a part of your daily routine.** Exercise is a needed release for your body and your brain. Prioritize and integrate it into your day, just like eating or taking medication.

- **Make your goals realistic.** We caution you not to freak out about exercise because you might get overwhelmed and not do anything at all. Figure out what will reasonably fit in, even if it's ten minutes a day.

- **Get out in nature.** Getting outside is naturally uplifting. There's a peace in nature that can't be replaced. Go soak up your vitamin D and go for a walk, do some gardening, take your dog to the park, or have some sort of adventure in the great outdoors. It will boost your mood!

- **Identify possible barriers.** This could be anything from budget to time constraints. Find a workaround such as working out at home, engaging in five-minute intervals per hour, or recruiting an accountability buddy.

- **Be mindful.** Exercise can be a respite from our chaotic lives if we are present and focus on the environment and physical sensations. For example, focus on the wind on your face or the sound of your shoes on the pavement.

- **Setbacks happen—accept it.** Setbacks come in all shapes and sizes. Keep in mind that they are a part of life. Think of all the micro-movements you've made toward integrating exercise into your life. *Focus on that*, not the setbacks.

We know getting into an exercise routine can be frustrating, especially if you have health issues. That doesn't let you off the hook, though. Find *something* that works for you, even if it is small. Get two-pound weights, and lift a few sets as you get ready in the morning. Have a resistance band at work, and squeeze in some reps when you listen in on a conference call. Buy a secondhand exercise bike or treadmill. Join a gym, go to physical therapy, or enlist the kids or pets for walks. Anything you can do to gradually build up your number of positive movements every day. Park your car across the lot to increase your steps into the office or store, take the stairs, or walk around the building a few times at lunch. All this adds up, and your mind, body, and soul will thank you.

✳ It's Your Turn to Play, Explore, and Learn ✳

Three Small Movements

Set a goal to make three small daily movements toward better eating and exercise. That might be something like:

- I'll eat a healthy breakfast every day this week.

- I will buy a probiotic and start taking it this week.

- I will increase my movements every day this week, such as parking farther from my destination, doing a five-minute YouTube exercise video every hour at work, and taking breaks for short walks.

- I will increase my intake of fruits and veggies every day this week to one fruit and one veggie every day!

- I will drink a water bottle every two hours this week during my day.

Mindful Eating

Commit to mindfully eating your food *once daily*, not just mindlessly shoving it on the go. We're often so busy that we eat on the run, in our car, in front of the TV, or at our desks. Make a conscious decision to tune into your sensations while eating at least once a day. Here are some steps to get you started:

- The first thing you want to do is take a few deep breaths. Notice stuff about your food, such as the color, texture, smell, or presentation.

- Be mindful of your intention to begin eating, such as *I am going to unwrap my food*, *I am going to use silverware*, or *I am opening the container*.

- As you bring the food to your mouth, notice how you anticipate the taste.

- When you take a bite, how does the food feel in your mouth? Chew slowly. What tastes are you experiencing? Are there a few tastes at once?

- As you continue eating, keep noticing all the sensations. When do you start feeling full? Really slow down and be aware of your movements, such as your hand bringing the food to your mouth, putting your fork down in between bites, and the sensations in your mouth.

✴ Quotes That Support This Mantra and Inspire ✴

- "Hell, If I had known I was going to live this long, I would have taken better care of my body."
  —Beth's dad

- "I believe depression is legitimate. But I also believe that if you don't exercise, eat nutritious food, get sunlight, get enough sleep,

consume positive material, surround yourself with support, then you aren't giving yourself a fighting chance."
  —Jim Carrey

- "Love yourself enough to live a healthy lifestyle."
  —Jules Robson

- "Take care of your body. It's the only place you have to live in."
  —Jim Rohn

- "Movement is a medicine for creating change in a person's physical, emotional and mental states."
  —Carol Welch

✷ Alternate Mantra Ideas for This Topic ✷

- A healthy outside starts with a healthy inside.

- Food affects my mood.

- Exercise lifts a weight off my shoulders.

- Why be moody when you can shake yo booty?

- Movement is medicine.

✷ Songs to Add to Your Mind Body Mantra Playlist ✷

- "Gonna Make You Sweat (Everybody Dance Now)"
  by C+C Music Factory

- "I Like It, I Love It"
  by Tim McGraw

- "Lose Yourself"
  by Eminem

- "The Eye of the Tiger"
  by Survivor

- "Move Your Body"
    by Sia

✳ Further Resources ✳

- *Unfuck Your Body: Using Science to Eat, Breathe, Move, and Feel Better*
    by Faith G. Harper

- *The Mind-Gut Connection: How the Hidden Conversation Within Our Bodies Impacts Our Mood, Our Choices, and Our Overall Health*
    by Emeran Mayer, MD

- *This Is Your Brain on Food: An Indispensable Guide to the Surprising Foods that Fight Depression, Anxiety, PTSD, OCD, ADHD, and More*
    by Uma Naidoo, MD

- *Built from Broken: A Science-Based Guide to Healing Painful Joints, Preventing Injuries, and Rebuilding Your Body*
    by Scott Hogan, CPT, COES

- *Perfect Health*
    by Deepak Chopra, MD

Acknowledgments

We'd like to acknowledge each and every person who believed in us along the way and encouraged us to keep going. We can't tell you how grateful we are for those generous and honest people who took time out of their lives to read a few of our chapters. The feedback you provided was amazing! To name a few, Betsy Torrens, Brenda Tanguay, Rosalia Ilic, Carole Dikinson, and Amelia Videan. Also, to our publisher, John Koehler, you are a kindred spirit with your laughter and positivity. And to our editor and designers, Miranda Dillon, Catherine Herold, and Lauren Sheldon, your invaluable guidance is so appreciated!

SOURCES BY CHAPTER

Part I: The Art and Science of Choosing Your Thoughts

"A Brief History of the Idea of Critical Thinking." n.d. www.criticalthinking.org. https://www.criticalthinking.org/pages/a-brief-history-of-the-idea-of-critical-thinking/408#:~:text=Socrates%20set%20the%20agenda%20for.

Amen, Daniel G. 2012. *Change Your Brain, Change Your Body : Use Your Brain to Get the Body You Have Always Wanted.* London: Piatkus.

Altman, D. 2010. *The Mindfulness Code: Keys for Overcoming Stress, Anxiety, Fear, and Unhappiness.* New World Library.

Blair, G. R. 2010. *Everything Counts! : 52 Remarkable Ways to Inspire Excellence and Drive Results.* Wiley.

Bohm, D. 2014. *On Dialogue.* Routledge.

Buonoman, Dean. 2011. *Brain Bugs: How The Brain's Flaws Shape Our Lives.* New York, NY: W.W. Norton & Company Inc.

Burns, D. D. 2017. *Feeling Good : The New Mood Therapy.* Blackstone Audio, Incorporated.

Brown, B. 2017. *Rising Strong : How the Ability to Reset Transforms the Way We Live, Love, Parent, and Lead.* Random House.

Chopra, Deepak, & Simon, David (2001). *Grow Younger, Live Longer.* New York, NY: Harmony Books.

"Cognitive Distortions: 10 Examples of Distorted Thinking." 2019. Healthline. December 18, 2019. https://www.healthline.com/health/cognitive-distortions#thought-origins.

Cushnir, Raphael 2008. *The One Thing Holding You Back: Unleashing The Power Of Emotional Connection.* New York, NY: HarperCollins Publishers.

Diener, Ed & Biawas-Diener, Robert. 2008. *Happiness: Unlocking the Mysteries of Psychological Wealth.* Malden, MA: Blackwell Publishing.

Dunn, D. 2018. Positive psychology : established and emerging issues. Routledge, An Imprint Of The Taylor & Francis Group.

Epstein, Mark 1995. *Thoughts Without a Thinker: Psychotherapy From a Buddhist Perspective.* New York, NY: Basic Books.

Farina, Cynthia R., Paul Miller, Mary J. Newhart, Claire Cardie, Dan Cosley, and Rebecca Vernon. 2011. "Rulemaking in 140 Characters or Less: Social Networking and Public Participation in Rulemaking." Pace Law Review 31 (1): 382. https://doi.org/10.58948/2331-3528.1772.

Fogel, S. J., & Rosin, M. B. 2014. *Your mind is what your brain does for a living : learn how to make it work for you.* Greenleaf Book Group Press.

Gilmore Crosby. 2015. *Fight, Flight, Freeze: Taming Your Reptilian Brain and Other Practical Approaches to Self-Improvement.* New York, NY, Eloquent Books, 2008.

Gough, E. 2021. *Making a Mantra : Tantric Ritual and Renunciation on the Jain Path to Liberation.* University of Chicago Press.

Hecht, Jennifer Micheal 2007. *The Happiness Myth: Why What We Think is Right is Wrong.* New York, NY: Harper Collins Press.

Hölzel, Britta K., James Carmody, Mark Vangel, Christina Congleton, Sita M. Yerramsetti, Tim Gard, and Sara W. Lazar. 2011. "Mindfulness Practice Leads to Increases in Regional Brain Gray Matter Density." *Psychiatry Research:*

Neuroimaging 191 (1): 36–43. https://doi.org/10.1016/j.pscychresns.2010.08.006.

Kabat-Zinn, J. 2004. *Wherever you go, there you are.* Piatkus.

Larson, Gary. *Damned If You Do, Damned If You Don't*, 1985. Universal Press Syndicate.

Le Bihan, D., & Fagan, T. L. 2015. *Looking Inside the Brain : The Power of Neuroimaging.* Princeton University Press.

Mapes, James. J. 2003. *Quantum Leap Thinking: An Owner's Guide to the Mind.* Naperville, Illinois: Sourcebooks, Inc.

Murre, Jaap M. J., and Joeri Dros. 2015. "Replication and Analysis of Ebbinghaus' Forgetting Curve." Edited by Dante R. Chialvo. *PLOS ONE* 10 (7). https://doi.org/10.1371/journal.pone.0120644.

Nelson, P. 2012. *There's a Hole in My Sidewalk.* Simon and Schuster.

Schwartz, J., & Beyette, B. 1997. *Brain Lock: Free Yourself From Obsessive-Compulsive Behavior.* Regan Books.

Seung, Sebastian, 2012. *Connectome: How the Brain's Wiring Makes Who We Are.* New York, NY: Houghton Mifflin Publishing Company.

Strayed, C. 2012. *Wild: From Lost To Found On The Pacific Crest Trail.* Alfred A. Knopf.

Sutton, Jeremy. 2020. "Socratic Questioning in Psychology: Examples and Techniques." Positive Psychology. June 19, 2020. https://positivepsychology.com/socratic-questioning/.

Taylor, Eldon 2009. *Mind Programming: From Persuasion and Brainwashing to Self-Help and Practical Metaphysics.* Carlsbad, CA: Hay House, Inc.

"The Power of Thoughts and Feelings—Fiona Muller | M1 Psychology." n.d. https://m1psychology.com/

the-power-of-thoughts-and-feelings/#:~:text=When%20we%20 intentionally%20and%20deliberately.

Tolle, Eckhart. 2000. *The Power of Now : A Guide to Spiritual Enlightenment*. Sydney., Nsw: Hodder Headline Australia.

Part II: Mantras for Everyday Obstacles
Rainy Day Mantras
Topic—Perfection / Mantra—Imperfection is Beauty

"3 Types of Perfectionism to Watch out for | Psychology Today." n.d. www.psychologytoday.com https://www. psychologytoday.com/us/blog/trust-yourself/202109/ 3-types-perfectionism-watch-out.

"25 Marisa Peer Quotes to Unleash Your Potential." 2022. Our Mindful Life. March 29, 2022. https://www.ourmindfullife. com/marisa-peer-quotes/. Accessed 11 Jan. 2024.

Alcott, Louisa May. (1868) 1989. *Little Women*. New York: Baronet Books.

Brown, Brene. 2010. *The Gifts of Imperfection*. Center City, Minn.: Hazelden.

Drive, Emerson. 2006. *I've Had My Moments*. Teddy Gentry and Josh Leo.

Evans, Sara. 2003. *Perfect*. Sara Evans and Paul Worley.

Nelsen, J. 2008. *Serenity: Simple Steps for Recovering Peace of Mind, Real Happiness, and Great Relationships*. Conari Press.

Ruiz, Miguel. 1997. *The Four Agreements: A Practical Guide to Personal Freedom*. San Rafael, Ca, Amber-Allen.

Tennant, Ella. 2022. "How the Philosophy behind the Japanese Art Form of _kintsugi_ Can Help Us Navigate Failure." The Conversation. November 8, 2022. https://theconversation.

com/how-the-philosophy-behind-the-japanese-art-form-of-kintsugi-can-help-us-navigate-failure-193487.

Topic—Positive Self-Concept / Mantra—Believe

"A Badass, Truth-Soaked Manifesto to Help Us Live like We Really Mean It. | Elephant Journal." 2016. Elephant Journal | Daily Blog, Videos, E-Newsletter & Magazine on Yoga + Organics + Green Living + Non-New Agey Spirituality + Ecofashion + Conscious Consumerism=It's about the Mindful Life. April 8, 2016. https://www.elephantjournal.com/2016/04/a-badass-truth-soaked-manifesto-to-help-us-live-like-we-really-mean-it/.

Bishop, Gary John. 2017 *Unfu*K Yourself.* HarperCollins.

Breathnach, Sarah Ban & McBain, E. 2014. *Something More.* Warner Books (NY).

Carlson, R. 1997. *Don't Sweat The Small Stuff- and it's All Small Stuff : Simple Ways to Keep the Little Things from Taking Over Your Life.* Hyperion.

Frankl, Viktor E, Daniel Goleman, and Franz Vesely. 2020. *Yes to Life: In Spite of Everything.* Boston: Beacon Press.

Henson, Jim, and Kermit The Frog. 1970. It Isn't Easy Bein' GreenSesame Street. Edited by Joe Rasposo. https://youtu.be/51BQfPeSK8k?si=ySG-Dxaoaq4kBPcY.

"Jim Carrey | Characters, Comedy, and Existence | TIFF Long Take." n.d. Www.youtube.com. https://www.youtube.com/watch?v=LMnrH1CN4oc.

Kempis, T. A. 2008. *The Imitation of Christ.* Catholic Book Publishing Corporation.

Markway, Barbara G, and Celia Ampel. 2018. *The Self-Confidence Workbook : A Guide to Overcoming Self-Doubt and Improving Self-Esteem*. Emeryville, Ca: AltheaPress.

Mcleod, Saul. 2023. "Normative & Informational Social Influence | Psychology." Simply Psychology. May 25, 2023. https:// www.simplypsychology.org/ Normative-informational-social-influence.html.

Perls, Friedrich Solomon, Ralph F Hefferline, and Paul Goodman. (1951) 2013. *Gestalt Therapy : Excitement and Growth in the Human Personality.* London Souvenir Press.

Robbins, M. 2009. *Be Yourself, Everyone else is Already Taken : Transform your Life with the Power of Authenticity*. Jossey-Bass.

Sincero, Jen. 2017. *You Are a Badass : [How to Stop Doubting Your Greatness and Start Living an Awesome Life]*. New York: Running Press, An Imprint Of Perseus Books, Llc.

Taylor, E. 2009. *Mind Programming*. Hay House, Inc.

Theole, Sue Patton. 2022. *The Courage to Be Yourself.* Mango Media Inc.

Zukav, Gary, and Linda Francis. 2012. *Heart of the Soul*. Simon and Schuster..

Topic—Perfectionism / Mantra—Humor is Healing

"Association for Applied and Therapeutic Humor | United States." 2017. AATH.org. 2017. https://www.aath.org/.

Kataria, Dr Madan. n.d. "Laughter Yoga International—Health, Happiness and World Peace." Laughter Yoga International. https://www.laughteryoga.org/.

Klein, A. 1989. *The Healing Power of Humor.* TarcherPerigee.

Laroche, L. 2004. *Life is Short, Wear Your Party Pants*. Hay House, Inc.

Nuar Alsadir. 2022. *Animal Joy: A Book of Laughter and Resuscitation*. Graywolf Press.

"What Is Laughter Yoga? | the Benefits of Laughter Yoga." 2007. Yoga Journal. October 25, 2007. https://www.yogajournal.com/lifestyle/laughter-cure/.

Topic—Rediscovering Your Curiosity / Mantra—Be Curious

Compton, William C, and Edward Hoffman. 2020. *Positive Psychology : The Science of Happiness and Flourishing*. Thousand Oaks, California, Sage Publications, Inc.

"Curiosity Is a Key to Well-Being | Psychology Today." n.d. www.psychologytoday.com. https://www.psychologytoday.com/us/blog/healthy-minds/202301/curiosity-is-a-key-to-well-being.

Kashdan, Todd B., Paul Rose, and Frank D. Fincham. 2004. "Curiosity and Exploration: Facilitating Positive Subjective Experiences and Personal Growth Opportunities." *Journal of Personality Assessment* 82 (3): 291–305. https://doi.org/10.1207/s15327752 jpa8203_05.

"Six Surprising Benefits of Curiosity." *Greater Good*, https://greatergood.berkeley.edu/article/item/six_surprising_benefits_of_curiosity#:~:text=Research%20has%20shown%20curiosity%20to,and%20greater%20psychological%20well%2Dbeing.

Topic—Inner Strength / Mantra—You Can Do Hard Things

Blades, Robin. 2021. "Protecting the Brain against Bad News." *CMAJ* 193 (12): E428–29. https://doi.org/10.1503/cmaj.1095928.

Huff, Charlotte. 2022. "Media Overload Is Hurting Our Mental Health. Here Are Ways to Manage Headline Stress." Apa.

org. American Psychological Association. November 1, 2022. https://www.apa.org/monitor/2022/11/strain-media-overload.

Raypole, Crystal. 2021. "Ready, Set, Journal! 64 Journaling Prompts for Self-Discovery." Psych Central. May 17, 2021. https://psychcentral.com/blog/ready-set-journal-64-journaling-prompts-for-self-discovery.

Schneiderman, Kim. 2015. *Step out of Your Story*. New World Library.

Toubiana, Madeline, Trish Ruebottom, and Luciana Turchick Hakak. 2022. "When a Major Life Change Upends Your Sense of Self." Harvard Business Review. January 28, 2022. https://hbr.org/2022/01/when-a-major-life-changeupends-your-sense-of-self.

Wendt, Taylor. 2022. "Amygdala: What to Know." WebMD. September 1, 2022. https://www.webmd.com/brain/amygdala-what-to-know.

Mantras That Encourage Letting Go

Stedman, M. L., & Gower, N. 2018. *The Light Between Oceans*. Penguin Books.

Topic—Letting Go and Living Simply / Mantra—If it's Not OK, it's Not the End

https://www.facebook.com/verywell. n.d. "Why Letting Go of Control Can Help You Enjoy Life." Verywell Mind. https://www.verywellmind.com/letting-go-of-control-can-help-you-enjoy-life-5208817#:~:text=How%20to%20Let%20Go%20Of%20Control%201%20Discern.

"Let Go of Control: How to Learn the Art of Surrender." 2015. Tiny Buddha. March 27, 2015. https://tinybuddha.com/blog/let-go-of-control -how-to- learn-the-art-of-surrender/.

Rabner, Jonathan, Nicholas D. Mian, David A. Langer, Jonathan S. Comer, and Donna Pincus. 2017. "*The Relationship between Worry and Dimensions of Anxiety Symptoms in Children and Adolescents.*" Behavioural and Cognitive Psychotherapy 45 (2): 124–38. https://doi.org/10.1017/S1352465816000448.

"Tiny Buddha: Wisdom Quotes, Letting Go, Letting Happiness In." *Tiny Buddha*, tinybuddha.com/.

Zelinski, Ernie J. 1998. *The Joy of Thinking Big: Becoming a Genius in No Time Flat.* Berkeley, Calif., Ten Speed Press.

Topic—Perceptions / Mantra—Assumptions are Assholes

Bailey, Rebecca Anne. 2001. *Conscious Discipline : 7 Basic Skills for Brain Smart Classroom Management.* Oviedo, Florida, Conscious Discipline.

Diener, Ed, and Robert Biswas-Diener. 2011. *Happiness.* John Wiley & Sons.

Kahn, M. 2020. *Whatever Arises, Love That.* Sounds True.

Loftus, E. F. 1975. Leading questions and the eyewitness report. *Cognitive Psychology*, 7(4), 560–572. https://doi.org/10.1016/0010-0285(75)90023-7.

Nelson, Jane 2008. *Serenity: Simple Steps for Recovering Peace of Mind, Real Happiness and Great Relationships.* San Francisco, CA: Red Wheel/Weiser LLC.

Pattakos, Alex 2004. *Prisoners of Our Thoughts: Viktor Frankl's Principles at Work.* San Francisco, CA: Berrett-Koehler Publishers, Inc.

Ziglar, Zig & Mayton, A. 2013. *See You At the Top*. Pelican Pub.

Topic—Acceptance / Mantra—Let Reality Be Reality

Alman, Brian 2011. *The Voice: Overcome Negative Self-Talk and Discover Your Inner Wisdom*. New York, NY: Sterling Publishing Company.

Beattie, Melody. 2009. *The Language of Letting Go*. Beverly Hills, Ca, Phoenix Audio.

Kübler-Ross, E., & Kessler, D. 2005. *On Grief & Grieving: Finding the Meaning of Grief Through the Five Stages of Loss*. Simon & Schuster.

Loveless, Patty. "How Can I Help You Say Goodbye?," Track 10 on Only What I Feel, EPIC Records, 1994, compact disc.

Vitale, J., & Haleakalā Hew Len. 2009. *Zero Limits : The Secret Hawaiian System For Wealth, Health, Peace, and More*. Wiley; Chichester.

"Welcome to Holland—Emily Perl Kingsley." n.d. Emily Perl Kingsley. https://www.emilyperlkingsley.com/welcome-to-holland.

Topic—Forgiveness / Mantra—Forgive and Make Room

American Psychiatric Association. 2019. "Patients & Families." Psychiatry.org. 2019. https://www.psychiatry.org/patients-families.

gabbyjamesonlineteacher. 2021. "31 Forgiveness Journal Prompts for Healing." Gabby James. December 7, 2021. https://gabbyjames.com/forgiveness-journal-prompts/.

Kolmannskog, V. 2018. *The Empty Chair Tales from Gestalt Therapy*. Editorial: Milton Routledge.

Nauman. 2022. "10 Tried and True Journal Prompts for Forgiveness." The Mindful Page. November 21, 2022. https://themindfulpage.com/journal-prompts-for-forgiveness/.

O'Connor, Mary-Frances. 2022. *The Grieving Brain the Surprising Science of How We Learn from Love and Loss.* Canberra: HarperCollins Publishers.

Simon, Sidney B, and Suzanne Simon. 2009. *Forgiveness.* Grand Central Publishing; Reprint edition (January 1, 1990).

Smedes, L. B. (2007). *Forgive and Forget : Healing the Hurts We Don't Deserve.* Harperone.

Mantras to Inspire Action
Topic—Taking Action & Goal Setting / Mantra—Just Don't Stand Still

Haughey, Duncan. 2014. "A Brief History of SMART Goals." Project Smart. December 13, 2014. https://www.projectsmart.co.uk/smart-goals/brief-history-of-smart-goals.php.

Jeffers, Susan J. 2017. *Feel the Fear And Do It Anyway.* London, Vermilion.

Topic—Being Present & Mindful Meditations / Mantra—Leave Your Mind Behind

"Active Meditation: What It Is, Techniques, and How to Do It." 2022. Psych Central. January 25, 2022. https://psychcentral.com/health/active-meditation.

Bertone, Holly. 2020. "Which Type of Meditation Is Right for You?" Healthline. September 17, 2020. https://www.healthline.com/health/mental-health/types-of-meditation#focused-meditation.

Brach, Tara, "Letting Go of Controlling: The Path to Freedom, Part 1," January 31, 2024.written by Tara Brach, podcast, running time 56:01, https://www.tarabrach.com/pt1-letting-go-controlling-path-freedom/.

Kabat-Zinn, Jon. 2018. "This Loving-Kindness Meditation Is a Radical Act of Love." Mindful. November 8, 2018. https://www.mindful.org/this-loving-kindness-meditation-is-a-radical-act-of-love/.

McKay, Matthew & Sutker, Catherine. 2007. *Leave Your Mind Behind.* Oakland, CA: New Harbinger Publications, Inc.

Nash, Jo. 2019. "What Is Loving-Kindness Meditation? (Incl. 4 Scripts + Youtube Videos)." PositivePsychology.com. July 27, 2019. https://positivepsychology.com/loving-kindness-meditation/.

Nunez, Kirsten. 2020. "The Benefits of Progressive Muscle Relaxation and How to Do It." Healthline. August 10, 2020. https://www.healthline.com/health/progressive-muscle-relaxation.

Topic—Gratitude / Mantra—Focus on the Good

Boll, H. 2011. *The Collected Stories of Heinrich Boll.* Melville House.

Brown, B. 2021. *What Separates Privilege from Entitlement Is Gratitude.* Self-Published.

"Discover the Three Keys of Gratitude to Unlock Your Happiest Life!: Jane Ransom at TEDxChennai." 2012. YouTube Video. *YouTube.* https://www.youtube.com/watch?v=ewi0qlqrshE.

Frankl, V. E. 2006. *Man's Search for Meaning.* Beacon Press.

Frost, N. 2016. *Truths, half truths and little white lies.* Hodder & Stoughton.

Hecht, Jennifer Michae. 2008. *The Happiness Myth : The Historical Antidote to What Isn't Working Today.* Harperone.

Lyubomirsky, S. 2014. *The Myths of Happiness : What Should Make You Happy But Doesn't, What Shouldn't Make You Happy But Does*. Penguin Books.

Lyubomirsky, Sonja, Kennon M. Sheldon, and David Schkade. 2005. "Pursuing Happiness: The Architecture of Sustainable Change." *Review of General Psychology* 9 (2): 111–31. https://doi.org/10.1037/1089-2680.9.2.111.

Nash, Jo. 2015. "The 5 Founding Fathers and a History of Positive Psychology." PositivePsychology.com. February 12, 2015. https://positivepsychology.com/founding-fathers/.

Russell, B. 2009. Philosophy *Unpopular Essays*. Routledge, 57.

Singh, D., & D'Souza, A. E. 2003. *Health, Wealth and Happiness*. ECW Press.

Tremendousness. 2016. "The Science of Gratitude." YouTube Video. *YouTube*. https://www.youtube.com/watch?v=JMd1CcGZYwU.

Zukav, G., & Francis, L. 2012. *Heart Of The Soul*. Simon and Schuster.

Topic—Balance / Mantra—Mix It Up

"30 Best Andre Gide Quotes with Image | Bookey." n.d. Www.bookey.app. https://www.bookey.app/quote-author/andre-gide.

Benson, Kyle. 2017. "The Magic Relationship Ratio, according to Science." The Gottman Institute. The Gottman Institute. October 4, 2017. https://www.gottman.com/blog/the-magic-relationship-ratio-according-science/.

Csikszentmihalyi, Mihaly. 1990. *Flow: The Psychology of Optimal Experience*. New York, Harper and Row.

Kessler, David A. 2010. *The End of Overeating: Taking Control of the Insatiable North American Appetite*. McClelland and Stewart.

Rogers, C. 1980. *A Way of Being.* Houghton Mifflin Co.

Scott, Dylan. 2023. "The Surgeon General Says Loneliness Is as Deadly as Smoking." Vox. May 3, 2023. https://www.vox.com/policy/2023/5/3/23707936/surgeon-general-loneliness-epidemic-report.

Summers, Juana, Vincent Acovino, and Christopher Intagliata. 2023. "America Has a Loneliness Epidemic. Here Are 6 Steps to Address It." NPR. May 2, 2023. https://www.npr.org/2023/05/02/1173418268/loneliness-connection-mental-health-dementia-surgeon-general.

Sutton, Jeremy. 2020. "How to Apply the Wheel of Life in Coaching." Positive Psychology.com. July 29, 2020. https://positivepsychology.com/wheel-of-life-coaching/.

Watterson, B. 1996. *Calvin and Hobbes: It's a Magical World.* Kansas City, Missouri: Universal Press Syndicate.

Mantras About Self-Care
Topic—Self-Care / Mantra—Self-Care is Not Self-indulgence, it's Self-preservation

Bethune, Sophie. 2022. "Stress in America 2022." Apa.org. American Psychological Association. October 2022. https://www.apa.org/news/press/releases/stress/2022/concerned-future-inflation.

Brown, Stuart L, and Christopher C Vaughan. 2009. *Play: How It Shapes the Brain, Opens the Imagination, and Invigorates the Soul.* New York, Avery.

Cliff, Sophie. 2022. *Choose Joy.* Blue Star Press.

Heinrich Böll, and Leila Vennewitz. 1995. *The Stories of Heinrich Böll.* Evanston, Ill.: Northwestern University Press.

Kondo, Marie. 2015. *Life-Changing Magic : Spark Joy Every Day.* Random House Inc.

Lama, D., Tutu, D., & Douglas Carlton Abrams. 2016. *The Book of Joy.* Penguin.

People Freaked Out." NPR. January 29, 2023. https://www.npr.org/2023/01/29/1152149068/marie-kondo-revealed-shes-kind-of-given-up-on-being-so-tidy-people-freaked-out#:~:text=%22The%20ultimate%20goal%20is%20to.

"Self-Care vs Self-Indulgence, Mental Wellbeing | ThoughtFull." n.d. www.thoughtfull.world. Accessed February 16, 2024. https://www.thoughtfull.world/mental-health/self-care-vs-self-indulgence#:~:text=1.

Yang, Mary. 2023. "Marie Kondo Revealed She's 'Kind of given Up' on Being so Tidy.

Topic—Self-Compassion / Mantra—Include YOU in Kindness

Millman, Dan. 2000. *Everyday Enlightenment : The Twelve Gateways to Personal Growth.* Sydney: Hodder.

Neff, Kristin. 2011. *Self-Compassion : The Proven Power of Being Kind to Yourself.* New York: HarperCollins Publishers.

Neff, Kristin, and Christopher K Germer. 2018. *The Mindful Self-Compassion Workbook : A Proven Way to Accept Yourself, Build Inner Strength, and Thrive.* New York, NY: Guilford Press.

Topic—Breathwork / Mantra—Just Breathe, Damn It

"10 Breathing Exercises to Try: For Stress, Training & Lung Capacity." 2019. Healthline. April 9, 2019. https://www.healthline.com/health/breathing-exercise#humming-bee-breath.

Association, American Lung. n.d. "2020: The Year We Lost Our Breath." Www.lung.org. https://www.lung.org/blog/2020-breath.

Dr. Weil. 2019. "Breathing Exercises: Three to Try | 4-7-8 Breath | Andrew Weil, M.D." DrWeil.com. January 7, 2019. https://www.drweil.com/health-wellness/body-mind-spirit/stress-anxiety/breathing-three-exercises/.

Kabat-Zinn, Judson/. 2018. The Craving Mind : From Cigarettes to Smartphones to Love is Why We Get Hooked and How We Can Break Bad Habits. Yale Univ Pr.

Kumar, Karthik. 2021. "Why Do Navy SEALs Use Box Breathing?" MedicineNet. MedicineNet. November 18, 2021. https://www.medicinenet.com/why_do_navy_seals_use_box_breathing/article.htm.

Ma, Xiao, Zi-Qi Yue, Zhu-Qing Gong, Hong Zhang, Nai-Yue Duan, Yu-Tong Shi, Gao-Xia Wei, and You-Fa Li. 2017. "The Effect of Diaphragmatic Breathing on Attention, Negative Affect and Stress in Healthy Adults." *Frontiers in Psychology* 8 (874): 1–12. https://doi.org/10.3389/fpsyg.2017.00874.

Rama, Swami & Ballentine, Rudolph & Hymes, Alan. 1998. Science of Breath: A Practical Guide. Honesdale, PA: The Himalayan Institute Press.

Talbott, Shawn. 2007. *The Cortisol Connection: Why Stress Makes You Fat and Ruins Your Health and What You Can Do About It.* Alameda, CA: Hunter House, Inc.

Thich Nhat Hanh. 2021. *Stepping into Freedom.* Parallax Press.

Tolle, E. 2018. *The Power of Now : A Guide to Spiritual Enlightenment.* Hachette Australia.

Van Der Kolk, B. 2015. *The Body Keeps the Score : Brain, Mind, and Body in the Healing of Trauma by Bessel van der Kolk, MD | Key Takeaways, Analysis & Review.* Idreambooks Inc.

Wachab, J. (Host). (2023, August 21). The *Mind Body Green* [Audio podcast].

Weil, Andrew. 1999. *Breathing: The Master Key to Self Healing*. Sounds True.

Weinstein, Richard. 2004. *The Stress Effect*. New York: Avery; London.

Topic—Introspection / Mantra—Talk to Your Soul

Hamilton, David. 2011. "Think Yourself Positive." David R Hamilton PHD. June 29, 2011.https://drdavidhamilton.com/think-yourself-positive/#:~:text=As%20we%20change%20our%20minds.

Lally, Phillippa, Cornelia H. M. van Jaarsveld, Henry W. W. Potts, and Jane Wardle. 2010. "How Are Habits Formed: Modelling Habit Formation in the Real World." *European Journal of Social Psychology* 40 (6): 998–1009. https://doi.org/10.1002/ejsp.674.

Lyubomirsky, Ph.D., Sonja. "Random Acts of Kindness." 2018, Berkeley.edu.https://ggia.berkeley.edu/practice/practice_as_pdf/random_acts_of_kindness?printPractice=Y.

Sutton, Jeremy. 2018. "5 Benefits of Journaling for Mental Health." PositivePsychology.com. May 14, 2018. https://positivepsychology.com/benefits-of-journaling/.

Topic—Mind-Body Connection / Mantra—The Mind and Body: BFFs

"Are Oreos Addictive? Research Says Yes." n.d. ScienceDaily. https://www.sciencedaily.com/releases/2013/10/131015123341.htm.

Brewer, Judson, and Jon Kabat-Zinn. 2017. *The Craving Mind : From Cigarettes to Smartphones to Love—Why We Get Hooked and How We Can Break Bad Habits.* New Haven: Yale University Press.

DeAngelis, Tori. "That Salad Isn't Just Good for Your Nutrition —It May Help Stave off Depression." *Apa.org*, 2023, www.apa.org/monitor/2023/06/nutrition-for-mental-health-depression.

"Diet and Mental Health." n.d. Www.mentalhealth.org.uk. https://www.mentalhealth.org.uk/explore-mental-health/a-z-topics/diet-and-mental-health#:~:text=Eat%20the%20right%20balance%20of.

Hart, Patricia. 2019. "What Is the Mind-Body Connection?" Taking Charge of Your Health & Wellbeing. 2019. https://www.takingcharge.csh.umn.edu/what-is-the-mind-body-connection.

Magazine, Smithsonian, and Sarah Kuta. n.d. "Getting 'Hangry' Is Real, Science Suggests." Smithsonian Magazine. https://www.smithsonianmag.com/smart-news/hanger-is-real-science-suggests-180980382/#:~:text=For%20one%2C%20being%20hungry%20may.

Siegel, Bernie S. 2005. *101 Exercises for the Soul: Simple Practices for a Healthy Body, Mind and Spirit.* Novato, California: New World Library.

www.ingramcontent.com/pod-product-compliance
Lightning Source LLC
LaVergne TN
LVHW041917070526
838199LV00051BA/2650